Literacy Solutions Textbook

Solving Your Reading Problem

A Step by Step Student Companion for Primary and
High School Students

Janet K. Newman

Literacy Solutions Textbook: Solving Your Reading Problem
A Step by Step Student Companion for Primary and High School Students

Copyright © 2025 by Janet K. Newman

First Edition 2025

ISBN:
Hardcover: 978-1-998245-46-8
Paperback: 978-1-998245-45-1
Cover and book design by Kabrena L. Robinson
Published in Canada by Eva-Michelle & Family Publishing
www.evamichelleandfamily.com

This book is lovingly dedicated to the literacy groups I taught from 2018 to 2024 at Holmwood Technical High School, Christiana, Manchester, Jamaica, W.I.

The journey I shared with you has been the inspiration and driving force behind this book. It is a testament to the work we covered in class and reflects how your enthusiastic reception of the material led to a notable growth in your reading skills and overall competence.

Your dedication, curiosity, and passion brought this project to life, and I am deeply grateful for each of you. May this book honour the strength of our shared vision and the remarkable potential within you all.

With heartfelt gratitude and admiration,

ACKNOWLEDGEMENT
PREFACE
MEET THE AUTHOR
MESSAGE TO STUDENTS
MESSAGE TO TEACHERS

TABLE OF CONTENTS

ACTIVITIES

CUT-OUT PAGES:
WORD BUILDING ACTIVITY WITH ONSET CARDS
WORD BUILDING ACTIVITY WITH WORD FAMILY/RIMES

The Macron and The Breve (Diacritical Marks)

The macron and breve are symbols placed above vowels. They are basically used to change the sound of the vowel within a word.

Macron (¯)

Symbol: Ā, ā

The macron is used to show a long vowel sound.

Examples:

- māde: Indicates a long "a" sound, as in the word "made."
- rēpeat: Shows a long "e" sound, as in the word "repeat."
- īcon: Shows a long "a" sound, as in "apron."
- dōnut: Marks a long "o" sound, as in "donut."
- cūrious: Indicates a long "u" sound, as in "curious."

Breve (˘)

Symbol: Ă, ă

The breve is used to show a short vowel sound

Examples:

- căt: Shows a short "a" sound, as in the word "cat."
- běnch: Indicates a short "e" sound, as in "bench."
- hǐdden: Marks a short "i" sound, as in "hidden."
- rŏck: Shows a short "o" sound, as in "rock."
- cŭp: Indicates a short "u" sound, as in "cup."

The slashes // are also used in this book.

When a letter or sound is placed between them, they help learners focus on the pronunciation. The slashes are used to represent the phonemes of a language.

For example:

- /p/ represents the phoneme "p" as in the word "pat."
- /ă/ represents the short "a" sound as in "cat."

ACKNOWLEDGEMENT

I want to express my deepest gratitude to everyone who believed in me and offered encouragement, especially during moments when I doubted myself. Having a network of positive and supportive people truly makes all the difference.

First and foremost, I wish to thank my husband, John Newman, who has been my unfailing pillar of strength and a constant source of motivation. I am immensely grateful to my best friend, Rashida Pownall, for her assistance with editing, and to her husband, Marlon Pownall, for their steadfast encouragement in my efforts to leave a lasting legacy. My heartfelt thanks also go to Moya Francis for her incredible inspiration, always encouraging me to share my knowledge through writing.

My heartfelt gratitude goes to my former colleague and sister in Christ, Sherice Bromfield, whose own journey in publishing her book inspired me to take this step. Her support and encouragement gave me the confidence to move forward with this project.

I also extend special thanks to Paula Faulknor-Bryan, Head of the APSE Department at Holmwood Technical High School, for her invaluable guidance and support along the way.

To my sister, Olethea Lewis, I am deeply grateful for your unwavering belief in me and for always standing by my side. And to my dear friend Richard Clarke, thank you for your steadfast faith in me and for always being a source of encouragement.

To each of you, your belief in me and your words of encouragement have been vital in this journey. Your support has given me the strength and confidence to pour myself into this book, and for that, I am eternally grateful.

PREFACE

Welcome to the Literacy Solutions Student's Workbook, a helpful resource designed to provide students with the necessary tools to develop a strong foundation in literacy at the primary and secondary levels.

The journey of mastering literacy is a gradual process that involves several key components. This workbook covers a wide range of topics, starting with Phonemic Awareness. Students will learn to recognize and manipulate phonemes, the smallest units of sound that form the basis of spoken language. Through engaging exercises, they will practice Phoneme Manipulation and work with Nonsense Words to strengthen their understanding of phonetic structure.

Understanding the difference between Short and Long Vowel Sounds is key for accurate pronunciation and spelling. The exercises will help students identify and use these sounds correctly in various contexts. Reading activities are designed to improve fluency and comprehension, while Building Vocabulary sections will expand their word knowledge and usage.

Syllabication is another vital skill that aids in reading and spelling. Students will learn to break down words into syllables, making them easier to read and write. The workbook also addresses the three sounds of -ed, providing clarity on how to pronounce and use this common suffix. Spelling exercises will reinforce correct spelling patterns and rules, while sections on Suffixes and Prefixes will help students understand how these word parts modify meaning.

Vowel Digraphs and Diphthongs are covered in detail to ensure students can recognize and pronounce these complex vowel combinations.

Word Recognition activities will boost students' ability to quickly identify and read words, improving their overall reading efficiency.

Throughout the workbook, various other skill-building exercises are included to reinforce learning and ensure that students develop a well-rounded set of literacy skills.

This workbook is designed to be both educational and enjoyable, with a variety of activities that cater to different learning styles. Whether used in a classroom setting or for individual learning, it aims to make learning to read and write an engaging and rewarding experience.

We hope that this Literacy Workbook will become a valuable resource for students, teachers, and parents alike. By working through the exercises, students will gain confidence in their literacy abilities, setting them on the path to academic success and a lifelong love of reading and writing.

Happy learning!

MESSAGE TO STUDENTS

The Literacy Solutions Workbook contains a lot of reading materials and activities to assist you in learning to become a good reader. However, it is important for you to work closely with your teacher to fully grasp the concepts. At the back of the book you will find useful websites that provide you access to more information. These resources will help to deepen your understanding by offering additional explanations, engaging content, and opportunities for practice beyond the classroom.

MESSAGE TO TEACHERS

While the Literacy Solutions Workbook offers a variety of activities to assist students in learning to read, it does not guarantee success without supplemental resources. Additional research may be necessary, as students could face challenges beyond the scope of this book.

The workbook also links helpful websites with additional information, interactive content, further explanations, and opportunities for extra practice outside the classroom. It incorporates a range of engaging strategies designed to reinforce learning.

It's important to regularly assess the activities and learning outcomes achieved to ensure accountability for both you and the student.

MEET THE AUTHOR

Janet K. Newman

Janet K. Newman is an accomplished educator with a deep passion for teaching. She holds a Bachelor of Arts degree in History from Northern Caribbean University with a minor in English and a teaching diploma from Church Teachers' College in Mandeville, Jamaica, majoring in double option English. Janet's teaching journey began at the kindergarten level, where she nurtured young learners for five years before transitioning to grades one through three, where she taught for thirteen years. Her dedication to education took a profound turn after she earned her teaching diploma and began working at the high school level. It was here that she recognized the urgent need for literacy support, especially among students who struggled with traditional learning methods. For seven years, Janet focused on transforming the lives of her high school students, applying her resourceful, creative, and innovative teaching strategies to address their literacy challenges. Born in the quaint district of Bent Town in Commer Pen, St. Elizabeth, Jamaica, Janet has touched thousands of lives through her teaching career. Her passion for literacy led her to write this book, aimed at providing a systematic approach to teaching literacy. It specifically targets primary and high school students who may feel embarrassed by using kindergarten-level materials, offering them an age-appropriate yet effective pathway to mastering literacy skills.

PHONEMIC AWARENESS: IDENTIFYING LETTER SOUNDS
Scoring and Prompts

- Place a tick next to each correct answer that the student provides.
- If the student gives the wrong answer, put an X or write down their response.
- If the student says the letter name instead of the letter sound, prompt with: "That is the letter name. What is the sound of the letter?"
- If the student hesitates and does not continue, point to the next letter and ask: "What's the sound of this letter?"
- Mark any missed letters with **ML**

a		b		c		d		e	
f		g		h		i		j	
k		l		m		n		o	
		p		q		r			
		s		t		u			
		v		w		x			
			y		z				

Evaluation:

_____

_____

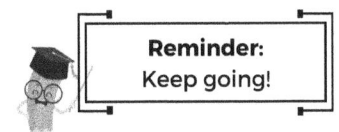

Reminder:
Keep going!

PHONEMIC AWARENESS SCREENER ASSESSMENT

Students must be asked to name the lowercase letters. Tick the letters that the student calls correctly. If the student calls the letter another name, write the letter of the name given in the circle. Evaluate the assessment in the space below.

a	◯	b	◯	c	◯	d	◯	e	◯
f	◯	g	◯	h	◯	i	◯	j	◯
k	◯	l	◯	m	◯	n	◯	o	◯
p	◯	q	◯	r	◯	s	◯	t	◯
u	◯	v	◯	w	◯	x	◯	y	◯
z	◯								

Evaluation:

_____

_____

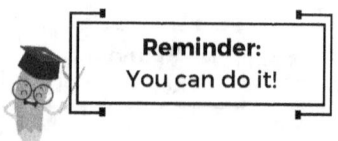

Reminder:
You can do it!

Teacher: Point to each vowel and say its short vowel sound.
Place a checkmark above the correct response.
Put an X if the answer is incorrect.

Start here and read across: **u** **e** **o** **i** **a**

Summative Evaluation:

_____
_____
_____
_____
_____
_____
_____
_____

What is your intervention plan for this student moving forward?

1. _____
_____
_____
_____

2. _____
_____
_____
_____

Time span of intervention plan: _____

PHONEME SEGMENTATION

Every word has letters. Letters are also called symbols.
These symbols or letters represent a sound.

Phoneme: A phoneme is the individual sound in a word.
A phoneme is represented like this: /m/
Example: The word **man** has three phonemes: /m/a/n/

Segmentation: Segmentation is breaking something into parts.
Example:

 **This is a segment of the pizza.**

Phoneme segmentation is breaking words into parts. That is, breaking words into individual sounds which are parts of a word.

Note: For more guidance, refer to the supplementary pages at the back of the book: **"Easy to Follow Rules for Phoneme Segmentation."**

Instructions: Look at each picture. Break the word into its individual sounds and write each sound in a separate box.
For example: **word:** bag **sounds:** /b/a/g/.

Word: red   **Sounds:** _____

Word: ant   **Sounds:** _____

Word: dog   **Sounds:** _____

Word: book   **Sounds:** _____

Word: basket   **Sounds:** _____

Word: table   **Sounds:** _____

Word: hands   **Sounds:** _____

Word: clock   **Sounds:** _____

Reminder:
Believe in yourself!

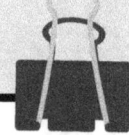

Instruction: The following words are segmented for you. Blend the sounds and tell which word. Write the word on the line.

Teacher: Tick the box if the student pronounces the word correctly. Put an X if the answer is incorrect.

Example: /w/i/n/d : _ _ _ _ _ _ **wind** _ _ _ _   ☑

- /p/a/r/t/y/ : _ _ _ _ _ _ _ _ _ _ _ _ _ _   ☐

- /l/o/g/ : _ _ _ _ _ _ _ _ _ _ _ _ _ _   ☐

- /s/t/a/n/d/ : _ _ _ _ _ _ _ _ _ _ _ _ _   ☐

- /j/u/g/ : _ _ _ _ _ _ _ _ _ _ _ _ _ _   ☐

- /l/a/s/t/ : _ _ _ _ _ _ _ _ _ _ _ _ _ _   ☐

- /r/o/ck/ : _ _ _ _ _ _ _ _ _ _ _ _ _   ☐

- /j/u/m/p/ : _ _ _ _ _ _ _ _ _ _ _ _ _ _ _   ☐

- /r/e/s/t/ : _ _ _ _ _ _ _ _ _ _ _ _ _   ☐

- /b/e/n/ch/ : _ _ _ _ _ _ _ _ _ _ _ _   ☐

- /b/l/i/n/k/ : _ _ _ _ _ _ _ _ _ _ _ _   ☐

PHONEME ADDITION

Remember: Phonemes are the individual sounds of the letters in a word. **Phoneme addition** is when you add a phoneme to the word that changes the word, the pronunciation and the meaning of the word.

Instruction: Add the given letter to the **beginning** of each word. Write the new word then call it for your teacher.

The word is **tar**. Add /s/
New word: _ _ _ _ _ _ _ _ _ _ _ _ _

The word is **ring**. Add /b/.
New word: _ _ _ _ _ _ _ _ _ _ _ _ _ _

The word is **mall**. Add /s/.
New word: _ _ _ _ _ _ _ _ _ _ _ _ _ _

The word is **ink**. Add /w/.
New word: _ _ _ _ _ _ _ _ _ _ _ _ _ _ _

The word is **end**. Add /t/.
New word: _ _ _ _ _ _ _ _ _ _ _ _ _ _

The word is **or**. Add /f/
New word: _ _ _ _ _ _ _ _ _ _ _ _ _ _

The word is **rum**. Add /d/
New word: _ _ _ _ _ _ _ _ _ _ _ _ _ _ _

The word is **runt**. Add /b/
New Word: _ _ _ _ _ _ _ _ _ _ _ _ _

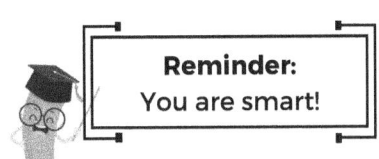

Reminder:
You are smart!

PHONEME SUBSTITUTION

Remember: Phonemes are the individual sounds of the letters in a word. To substitute means to take away. **Phoneme substitution** is taking away an individual sound in a word and replacing it with another.

Examples:

The word is **clap.** Replace the /c/ with /s/. The new word is **slap**

The word is **clap.** Change the /l/ to /r/. The new word is **crap**

The word is **tick.** Change the /i/ to /u/. The new word is **tuck**

Complete the following exercise.

The word is **black.** Change /b/ to /s/.

New word: _ _ _ _ _ _ _ _ _ _ _ _ _

The word is **hold.** Change /h/ to /b/.

New word: _ _ _ _ _ _ _ _ _ _ _ _ _ _

The word is **song.** Change /o/ to /a/.

New word: _ _ _ _ _ _ _ _ _ _ _ _ _ _

The word is **slim.** Change /s/ to /f/.

New word: _ _ _ _ _ _ _ _ _ _ _ _ _ _

The word is **rag.** Change /a/ to /u/.

New word: _ _ _ _ _ _ _ _ _ _ _ _ _ _

The word is **baby.** Change /y/ to /e/.

New word: _ _ _ _ _ _ _ _ _ _ _ _ _ _ _

The word is **alone.** Change /e/ to /g/.

New word: _ _ _ _ _ _ _ _ _ _ _ _ _ _ _

The word is **slit.** Change /l/ to /p/.

New word: _ _ _ _ _ _ _ _ _ _ _ _ _ _ _

The word is **hop.** Change /h/ to /s/.

New word: _ _ _ _ _ _ _ _ _ _ _ _ _ _ _

The word is **hunt.** Change /h/ to /r/.

New word: _ _ _ _ _ _ _ _ _ _ _ _ _ _ _

The word is **give.** Change /g/ to /l/

New word: _ _ _ _ _ _ _ _ _ _ _ _ _ _ _

The word is **hard.** Change /d/ to /m/.

New word: _ _ _ _ _ _ _ _ _ _ _ _ _ _ _

The word is **maid.** Change /ai/ to /u/.

New word: _ _ _ _ _ _ _ _ _ _ _ _ _ _ _

The word is **bud.** Change /u/ to /e/.

New word: _ _ _ _ _ _ _ _ _ _ _ _ _ _ _

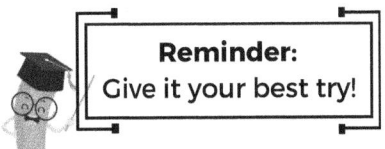

Reminder:
Give it your best try!

PHONEME DELETION

Deletion: Taking out something that was there before

Remember: Phonemes are individual sounds in a word.

Phoneme deletion: Taking out one of the sounds in a word.

Examples: The word is **duck.** Say it without the **/d/ = uck**

The word is **girl.** Say it without the **/r/ = gil**

Instruction: Complete the following using the examples above to help you.

Teacher: Put a checkmark in the box if the answer is correct.

☐ The word is **start.** Say it without the /s/   _ _ _ _ _ _ _ _ _ _ _ _ _ _ _ _ _

☐ The word is **window.** Say it without the /w/   _ _ _ _ _ _ _ _ _ _ _ _ _ _ _ _

☐ The word is **donkey.** Say it without the /d/   _ _ _ _ _ _ _ _ _ _ _ _ _ _ _ _

☐ The word is **work.** Say it without the /k/   _ _ _ _ _ _ _ _ _ _ _ _ _ _ _ _

☐ The word is **shame.** Say it without the /sh/   _ _ _ _ _ _ _ _ _ _ _ _ _ _ _ _

☐ The word is **bunny.** Say it without the /b/   _ _ _ _ _ _ _ _ _ _ _ _ _ _ _ _

PHONEME ISOLATION

> **Isolation:** Focusing on and identifying something specific.
>
> **Remember**: Phonemes are individual sounds of a word.
>
> **Phoneme isolation** is identifying a specific sound in a word.

Examples: The word is **rich.** What is the initial (first) sound in the word?
The word is **gold.** What is the final (last) sound in the word?
The word is **jet**. What is the medial (middle) sound in the word?

*Assessor should call the words.

What is the initial sound (Not the letter) in the word.		What is the medial sound (Not the letter) in the word.		What is the final sound (Not the letter) in the word.	
make	/m/	rain	/ā/	echo	/ō/
spin	/s/	ride	/ī/	war	/r/
king	/k/	deal	/ē/	clip	/p/
church	/ch/	get	/ĕ/	sound	/d/
thing	/th/	jam	/ă/	fill	/l/
idea	/ī/	hot	/ŏ/	cough	/f/
him	/h/	cute	/ū/	take	/k/

PHONEME BLENDING

Blending: To blend something is to put something together or combine things. By blending we get something new.

Remember: Phonemes are the individual sounds in a word.

Phoneme blending is identifying the individual sounds in a word, putting the sounds together and saying what the word is.

Examples: The sounds /a/ and /t/ when blended makes the word "at" and /f/l/a/t/ is "flat".

Instruction: Combine the sounds and pair the words with their matching pictures.

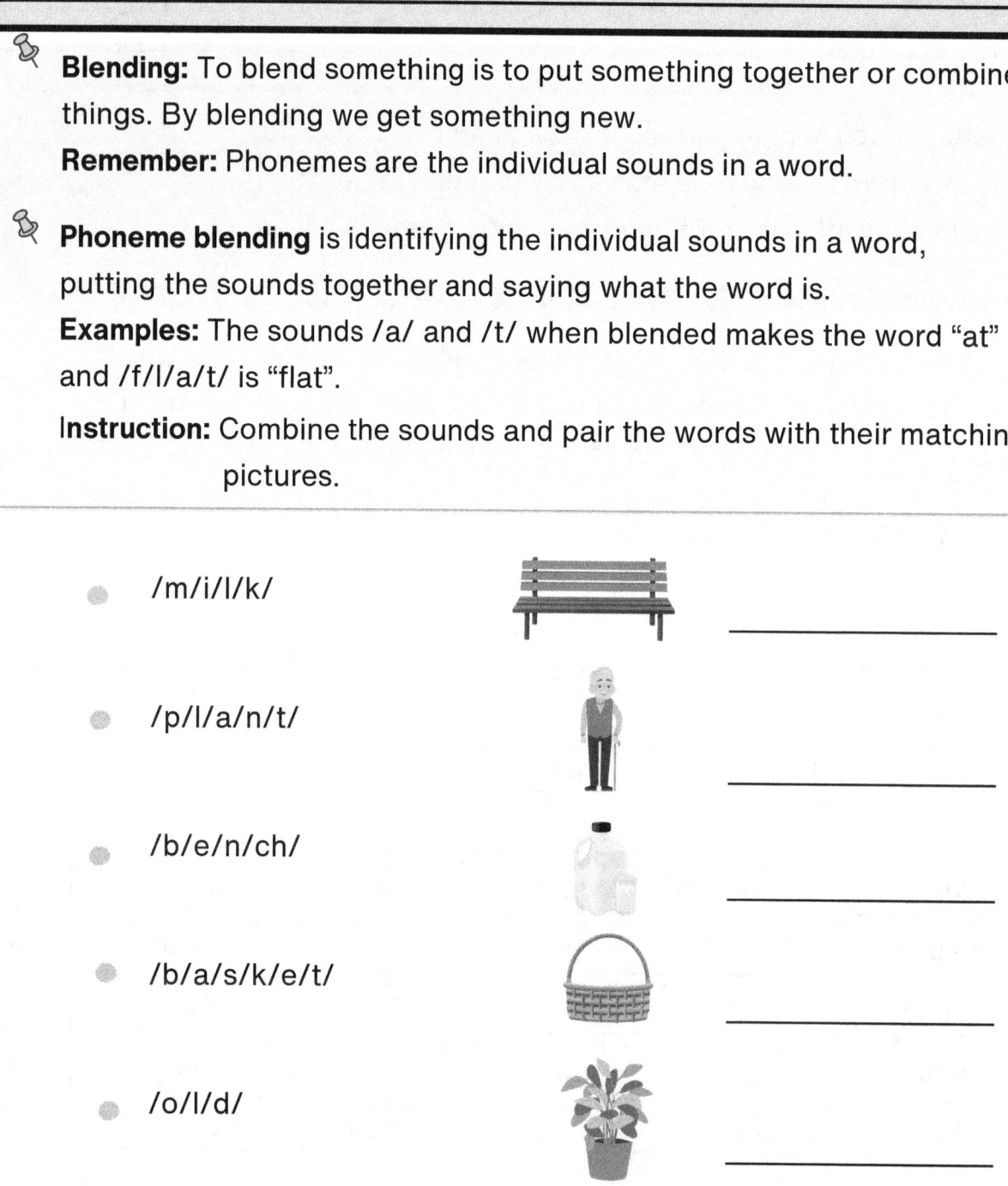

- /m/i/l/k/

  _____

- /p/l/a/n/t/

  _____

- /b/e/n/ch/

  _____

- /b/a/s/k/e/t/

  _____

- /o/l/d/

  _____

Instruction: Say what word you will get if you put each group of sounds together.

Teacher: Put a tick in the oval if the word is correct.

Example: /w/i/n/d/ : _ _ _ _ _**wind**_ _ _ _ _

/o/i/l/ _ _ _ _ _ _ _ _ _ _ _ _ _ _ _ _ _   ◯

/p/l/a/n/e/t/: _ _ _ _ _ _ _ _ _ _ _ _ _ _   ◯

/s/e/n/d/: _ _ _ _ _ _ _ _ _ _ _ _ _ _ _ _   ◯

/g/r/a/s/p/: _ _ _ _ _ _ _ _ _ _ _ _ _ _   ◯

/j/u/n/k/: _ _ _ _ _ _ _ _ _ _ _ _ _ _ _   ◯

/b/a/n/k/: _ _ _ _ _ _ _ _ _ _ _ _ _ _   ◯

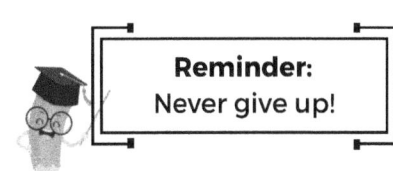

Reminder:
Never give up!

SINGLE SYLLABLE ONSET-RIME

📌 **Onset**: The first consonant sound, blend or digraph that you make in a word. It comes before the vowel sound.

📌 **Rime**: The vowel sound and other sounds that follow after the first consonant sound in the word.

📌 **Onset-Rime:** Dividing a syllable into two parts: the onset and the rime.
Example: **st** (onset) + **em** (rime) = stem

Before going into blending onset-rimes, it is important to go through the pronunciation of the letters so that you have a better handle on blending words.

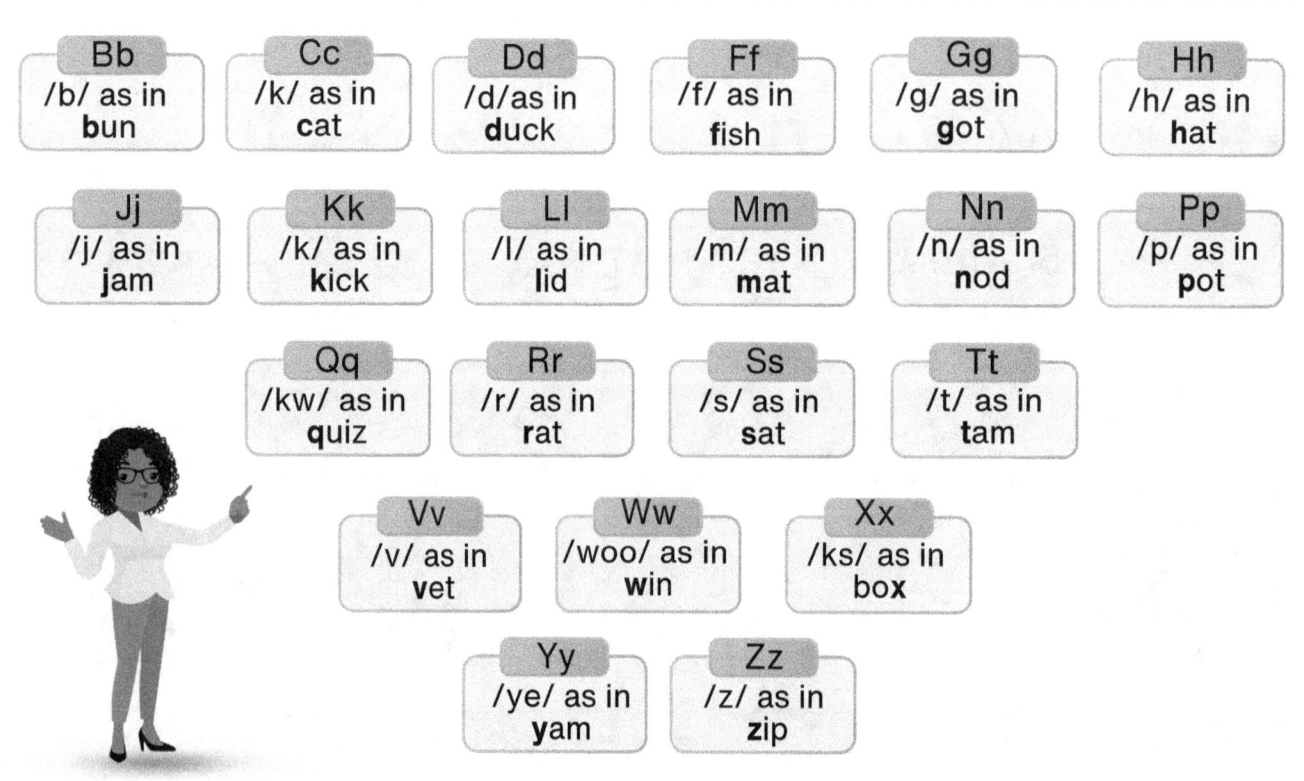

Bb	Cc	Dd	Ff	Gg	Hh
/b/ as in **bun**	/k/ as in **cat**	/d/ as in **duck**	/f/ as in **fish**	/g/ as in **got**	/h/ as in **hat**

Jj	Kk	Ll	Mm	Nn	Pp
/j/ as in **jam**	/k/ as in **kick**	/l/ as in **lid**	/m/ as in **mat**	/n/ as in **nod**	/p/ as in **pot**

Qq	Rr	Ss	Tt
/kw/ as in **quiz**	/r/ as in **rat**	/s/ as in **sat**	/t/ as in **tam**

Vv	Ww	Xx
/v/ as in **vet**	/woo/ as in **win**	/ks/ as in **box**

Yy	Zz
/ye/ as in **yam**	/z/ as in **zip**

Single Syllable Onset-Rime Blending

Vowel Sounds

There are five vowels in the alphabet, A, E, I, O and U. Y can sometimes function as a vowel when there is no other vowel in the word.

For example: why, rhythm.
It is also considered a vowel when it forms a dipthong, for example; ey as in monkey, ay as in day, oy as in toy.

Vowel sounds in the English language can either be long or short.

Short Vowel Sounds	Long Vowel Sounds
ă as in bat	ā as in rain
ĕ as in egg	ē as in eagle
ŏ as in orange	ī as in kite
ĭ as in bin	ō as in old
ŭ as in nut	ū as in unicorn
oo as in put	or blue

*The long "u" sound can be pronounced in two ways, depending on the word. It can either sound like "yoo" or a plain "oo."

Single Syllable Onset-Rime Blending Cont'd

Teacher: Ask the student to pronounce the onset then the rime. Ask the student to now blend them together.
Ask the student to write the word in column three.

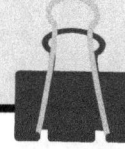

Onset	Rime	Blended Word
p	ast	
h	ill	
n	ot	
cr	ush	
w	ing	
h	unt	
sl	am	
f	ist	

Single Syllable Onset-Rime Blending Cont'd

Building Word Families

A word family consists of words that share the same ending (rime). We create word families by adding various onsets to the rime. (Begin by forming words using short vowel sounds.)

Example: **-and** is a *rime.* We can build word families by adding different onsets like **gr, h, l, st, b, r, br**

- gr + and = grand

- h + and = hand

- l + and = land

- st + and = stand

- b + and = band

- r + and = rand

- br + and = brand

Use the onsets above to build at least three words each with these families (rimes)

1. um: _____ _____ _____

2. end: _____ _____ _____

3. ill: _____ _____ _____

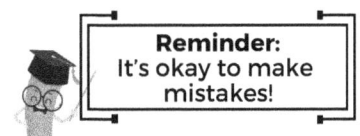

Reminder:
It's okay to make mistakes!

SHORT VOWEL SOUND PRACTICE- NONSENSE WORD EXPLORATION

 Nonsense words do not make sense, but, they allow for more sounds and sound combinations than real words. They also help you to rely on your decoding skills and not what is stored in your memory.

Instructions: Call the following nonsense words as you would your regular words.

Teacher: Tick the box if the student calls them correctly.

Exploration 1

baz		yev		zed	
zix		es		jeb	
luz		quil		sur	
yof		col		hor	
wob		zif		feh	
ib		cag		ol	
oy		kip		zuz	
baj		lig		jus	
caf		hec		dun	
tuf		ux		huf	
rus		mev			

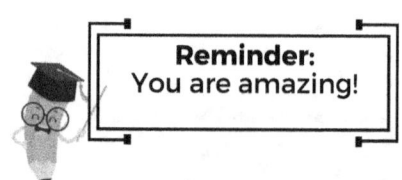

Reminder:
You are amazing!

Exploration 2

arb		nez		zipt	
welx		toft		ocks	
ux		zilp		nolt	
ifs		aft		jej	
og		nesh		rund	
og		luds		jows	
vars		kiks		arf	
wurf		omb		rind	
welp		hiv		reph	
zawd		ligs		uzt	
felf		zonk		asp	

Exploration 3

shez		wheg		spen	
glick		clid		snix	
bron		choz		skov	
trug		scub		cruf	
brin		krig		flax	
spif		swon		skas	
claz		broy		crim	
zlim		drav		spod	
cled		phos		gwen	
frib		shul		whuck	

SHORT VOWEL SOUND PRACTICE

Instruction: Look at each picture. Call the name of the picture. Write the vowel to complete the spelling of each word.

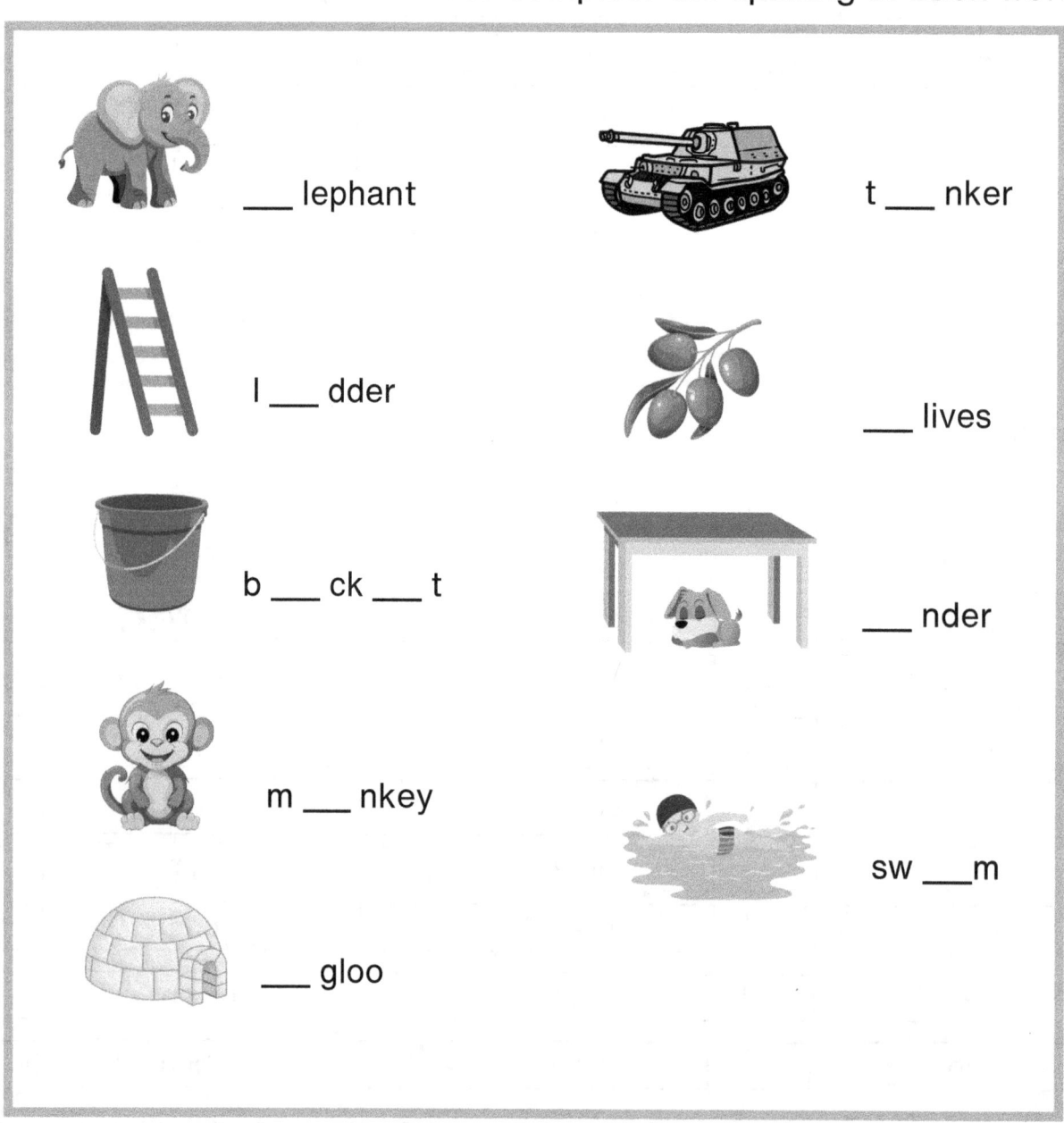

___ lephant

t ___ nker

l ___ dder

___ lives

b ___ ck ___ t

___ nder

m ___ nkey

sw ___ m

___ gloo

Short Vowel Sound Practice Cont'd

The Sun and Its Heat

The sun is a big, hot star. It sits up high in the sky. The sun gives us light and heat. Each day, the sun comes up at dawn. Its rays make the land warm. Plants need the sun to grow. If we stand in the sun, we feel warm. The sun sets at dusk and the sky gets dark. Then, the moon and stars come out. The sun helps life on Earth by giving us light and heat.

	Actual number	%
Number of words read		
Number of words incorrect		
Words Per Minute		

To calculate the percentage for the WPM, divide the actual number of words read by the total number of words in the passage then multiply it by 100.

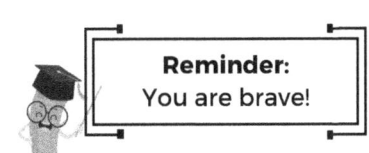

Reminder:
You are brave!

Short Vowel Sound Practice-
Spelling on the Stairs

Instruction: Write the letters of each word that the teacher calls step by step on the stairs as shown in the example below.

p						
p	l					
p	l	a				
p	l	a	n			
p	l	a	n	e		
p	l	a	n	e	t	
p	l	a	n	e	t	s

SPELLING ON THE STAIRS

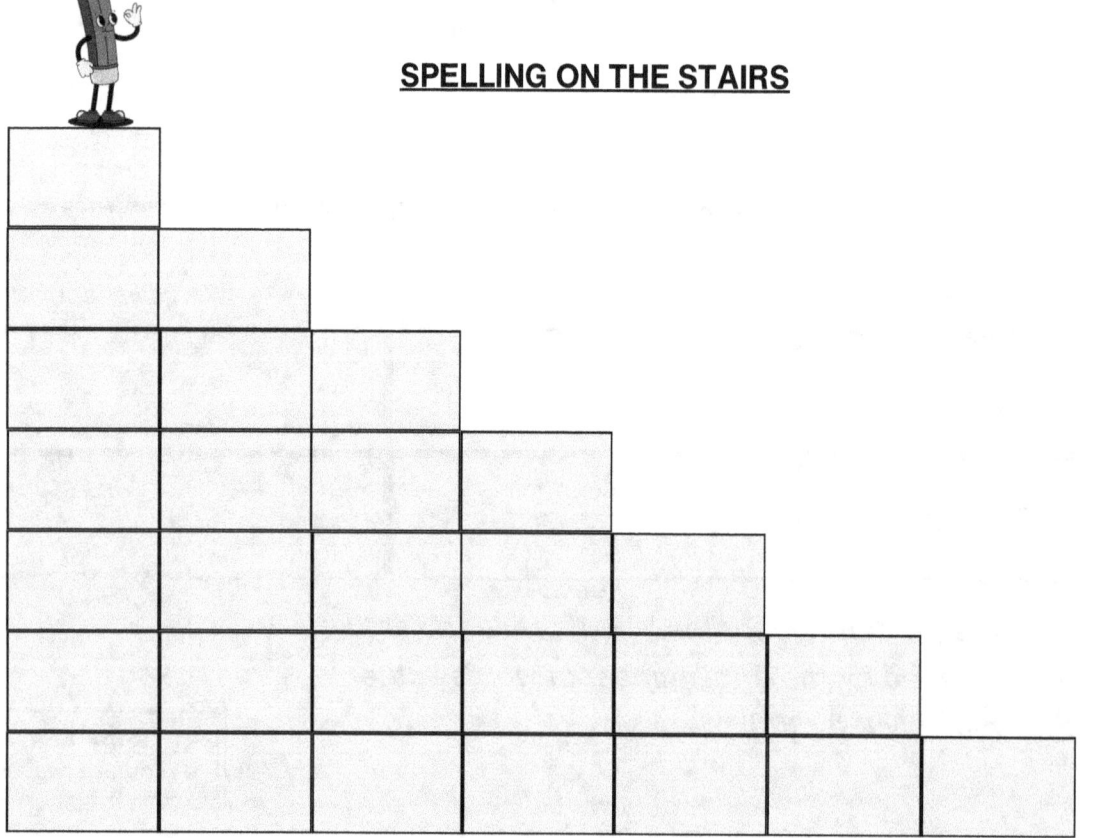

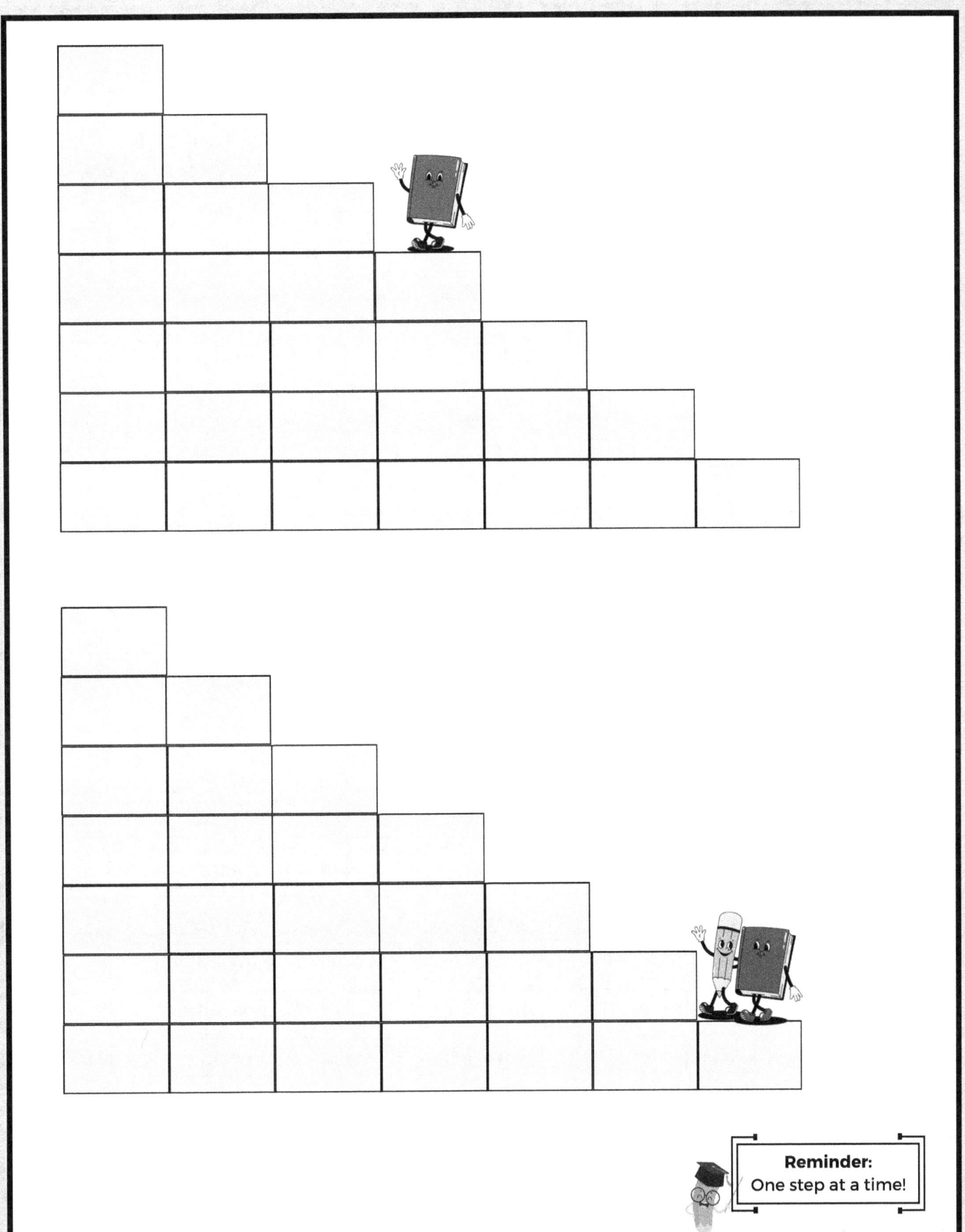

Pre-Primer—Grade 3 Sight Word List

Teacher: Ask student to call the list of sight words. Put a tick in the box of each correct answer. Put an X if the word is called incorrectly. This list by no means exhausts the number of sight words available. Feel free to add to it.

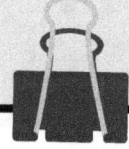

and		little		could	
children		over		never	
but		here		please	
laugh		under		only	
one		you		round	
between		both		about	
up		not		walk	
across		cannot		better	
we		my		take	
close		bought		show	
play		after		know	
baby		anything		carry	
see		stop		because	
with		keep		myself	
him		when		beautiful	
above		grow		good	

THE LONG VOWEL SOUND

 The long vowel sounds usually call their own name. There are different ways of making the long vowel sound.

1. **Pair a vowel with another vowel.** When we pair a vowel with another another vowel, we call them vowel digraphs. Example: ea, oa, ay, ie, ei, ue, ai, ey. Usually in this case, the first vowel does the talking.

2. **When the vowel e comes at the end of a word,** the penultimate vowel makes a long sound (VC-e). Example: ōre, ēme, ūne, īke, āpe

3. **If a vowel comes at the end of a syllable** (Open Syllable) the vowel can be open.
   Example: mu/sic, re/lax, o/pen, ba/by

1. **If I and O come before two consonants,** they will carry a long sound. Examples: kind, old.

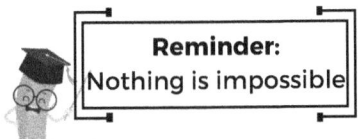

Reminder:
Nothing is impossible

Long 'a' Sound Words

a	ai	ay	a_e
acorn ☐	vain ☐	hay ☐	beware ☐
apron ☐	paid ☐	stay ☐	shade ☐
bacon ☐	waist ☐	today ☐	stage ☐
table ☐	wait ☐	away ☐	case ☐
crazy ☐	daily ☐	relay ☐	flame ☐
tomato ☐	grain ☐	spray ☐	space ☐
basic ☐	afraid ☐	tray ☐	waste ☐
bacon ☐	maid ☐	May ☐	lake ☐
paper ☐	aim ☐	holiday ☐	wade ☐
data ☐	tail ☐	bray ☐	crate ☐
baby ☐	braid ☐	pray ☐	cane ☐

ea	ei	ey	eigh
steak ☐	their ☐	prey ☐	neigh ☐
break ☐	beige ☐	grey ☐	weigh ☐
great ☐	vein ☐	they ☐	neighbour ☐
swear ☐	heir ☐	hey ☐	eight ☐
near ☐	rein ☐	obey ☐	weight ☐
bear ☐	reindeer ☐	survey ☐	freight ☐

Instruction: Create at least ten nonsense words in each column with the following long /a/ sound patterns. (These are three of the most common long A vowel teams.)

ai	ay	a_e

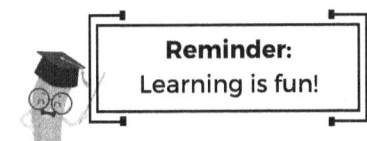

Reminder:
Learning is fun!

WORD RECOGNITION

Instruction: Identify the words in each column.

Mixed Pattern Words	Mixed Pattern Words	Nonsense Words
blaze ☐	heinous ☐	fraip ☐
train ☐	praise ☐	trame ☐
tailor ☐	raisin ☐	greigh ☐
razor ☐	apron ☐	smay ☐
freight ☐	fable ☐	lein ☐
later ☐	great ☐	craton ☐
brain ☐	their ☐	bave ☐
lazy ☐	state ☐	tabe ☐
stray ☐	stay ☐	faim ☐
rein ☐	weigh ☐	yase ☐

Total: _____/_____   Total: _____/_____   Total: _____/_____

Reminder:
Nothing is impossible

Long /a/ Sound Reading Passage

An Amazing Day at the Fair

It was an amazing day, and Layla couldn't wait to go to the fair. She had saved her money all month to pay for rides and games. As she walked down the main street, she could hear the band playing and see the bright lights of the Ferris wheel.

The first thing Layla did was race to the paint booth. There, she saw a rainbow of paints and brushes laid out in trays. "May I paint a picture?" she asked the lady at the booth. "Of course!" the lady said with a smile. Layla picked up a brush and began to create a picture of the fair.

Next, Layla wanted to play a game. She saw a booth where you could win a stuffed bear by aiming a ball at some pins. Layla paid the man at the booth and took aim. She threw the ball straight and knocked down all the pins! "Hooray!" she cheered as she won the biggest bear.

After that, Layla went to get some cake at the snack stand. The cake was sweet and tasty, just like she had hoped. She even saw a friend from school named Ray, and they decided to stay together for the rest of the day.

As the sun began to set, Layla saw a parade coming down the street. The parade was full of floats and dancers, all dressed in bright colours. Layla and Ray waved at the performers, and they waved back.
When it was time to go home, Layla felt tired but happy. She knew this was a day she would always remember. As she walked away, she thought about how much fun she had, and she couldn't wait for the fair to come back next year.

Number of long /a/ sound words from the passage: _ _ _ _ _ _ _ _ _ _ _

Number of words incorrect: _ _ _ _ /290

Percentage: _ _ _ _ _ _ _ _ _ _ _ _ _ _ _ _

Long /a/ Sound Reading Passage

A Day with Jake and Kate

Jake and Kate love to play all day. They wake up early and eat their breakfast. Then, they race to the yard to play.

Jake likes to play with his toy train. He makes the train go fast on the track. "Choo-choo!" says Jake as the train goes by.

Kate has a doll she named May. May has a pretty dress and a cute hat. Kate likes to play house with May. She pretends that May is having a big tea party.

Later, Jake and Kate find some crayons. They sit at the table and draw a big cake with candles. "This cake is for May's party!" says Kate. Jake helps to make the cake look bright and colourful.

At the end of the day, Jake and Kate are tired. They put away their toys and say goodnight to May. "Today was a fun day!" says Jake. "I can't wait to play again tomorrow," says Kate with a big smile.

Number of long /a/ sound words from the passage: _ _ _ _ _ _ _ _ _ _ _

Number of words incorrect: _ _ _ _/160

Percentage: _ _ _ _ _ _ _ _ _ _ _ _ _ _ _ _ _

Long /e/ Sound Words

e				
evil	even	equal	ego	economy

ee						
teeth	eel	meet	seem	sheet	feed	deer
wheel	needle	freeze	steel	keep	weed	queen
steep	heel	bee	need	seen	sleep	feeble
creep	cheese	free	green	sheen	steeple	

e_e						
eve	extreme	delete	these	interfere	precede	chinese
gene	complete	severe	even	concede	interfere	scene

ie						
thief	sieve	piece	niece	chief	mischief	believe
relief	brief	yield	grief	cookie	achieve	shield

Long /e/ Sound Words Cont'd

ey				
key	donkey	money	parsley	valley
turkey	honey	chimney	pulley	

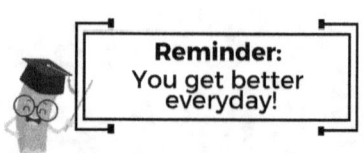

GRAPHEME & PHONEME CHARTING

📌 **Instruction: Listen to the word that the teacher calls.**

Example: The word is swift.

Tap out the sounds with your fingers

1 2 3 4 5

Say the Word	Tap out the sounds that you hear in the word				
Map the Sound Sound out the word and put a tick in the box for every sound that you hear	✓	✓	✓	✓	✓
Graph the Word Write the letter for each sound that you hear to spell the word. Write one sound in each box.	/S/	/w/	/i/	/f/	/t/
Write out the whole word	**swift**				

Grapheme & Phoneme Charting Cont'd

Instruction: Listen to the word that the teacher calls.

Say the Word	Tap out the sounds that you hear in the word				
Map the Sound Sound out the word and put a tick in the box for every sound that you hear					
Graph the Word Write the letter for each sound that you hear to spell the word. Write one sound in each box.					
Write out the whole word					

Grapheme & Phoneme Charting Cont'd

Instruction: Listen to the word that the teacher calls.

Say the Word	Tap out the sounds that you hear in the word				
Map the Sound Sound out the word and put a tick in the box for every sound that you hear					
Graph the Word Write the letter for each sound that you hear to spell the word. Write one sound in each box.					
Write out the whole word					

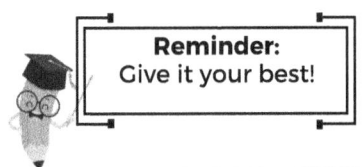

Reminder: Give it your best!

WORD RECOGNITION

Mixed Word Recognition Activity
Long e Sound

email ☐	diesel ☐	achieve ☐	weave ☐
evil ☐	thief ☐	leaf ☐	needle ☐
remain ☐	maybe ☐	compete ☐	redeem ☐
Eden ☐	beef ☐	yield ☐	trolley ☐
report ☐	heal ☐	donkey ☐	please ☐
before ☐	here ☐	valley ☐	bleach ☐

| TOTAL: | TOTAL: | TOTAL: | TOTAL: |

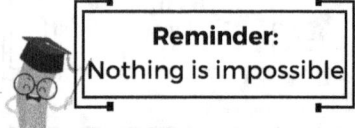

Reminder:
Nothing is impossible

Long /e/ Reading Passage

Pete The Bee

Pete the bee loves to fly from tree to tree. He sees the green leaves and the pretty flowers. Pete likes to eat sweet honey. Every day, he works with his bee friends to make more honey. They all sleep in a big beehive when the day is done. Pete is happy to help his friends and keep the flowers blooming.

Number of long e sound words from the passage: _ _ _ _ _ _ _ _ _

Long /e/ Sound Reading Passage

<u>Three Little Kittens</u>

Three little kittens set out on a great adventure. They wanted to see what was beyond the green hills near their home. As they walked, they found a deep stream where they could take a drink. The trees around them were tall and leafy, providing plenty of shade. The kittens felt free and happy as they explored the wide, open fields. When evening came, they made their way back, eager to share their exciting day with their family.

Number of long /e/ sound words from the passage:

– – – – – – – – – – –

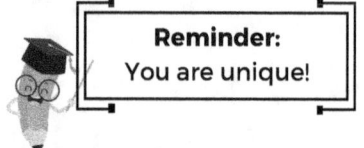

Reminder:
You are unique!

Long /e/ Reading Passage

Bees

Bees are essential creatures in our ecosystem. They are known for their ability to pollinate flowers, which is key to the growth of many plants. Without bees, we would see a decrease in the availability of fruits, vegetables, and seeds. Bees have a unique way of communicating, using a "waggle dance" to show the direction and distance to a food source. Despite their small size, bees play a significant role in maintaining the balance of nature. Protecting bees is vital to ensuring a healthy environment for future generations.

Number of long e sound words from the passage: _ _ _ _ _ _ _ _ _ _

Long /e/ Sound Reading Passage

Green Energy

Green energy is becoming increasingly important in the fight against climate change. Solar panels and wind turbines are two key technologies that generate electricity without releasing harmful emissions. By harnessing the power of the sun and wind, we can reduce our reliance on fossil fuels and decrease greenhouse gas emissions. Clean energy sources like these are essential for creating a sustainable future. Investing in green energy not only helps the environment but also creates new jobs in the renewable energy sector.

Number of long /e/ sound words from the passage: _ _ _ _ _ _ _ _ _

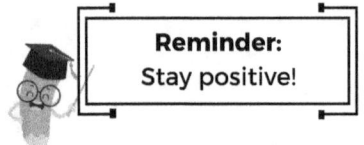

Reminder:
Stay positive!

Long /i/ Sound Words

i					
idol	tiny	shiny	tidy	spider	silent
pilot	iron	Bible	final	item	China
Friday	final	bicycle	quiet	library	shiloh

i_e						
hive	kite	site	rime	time	pine	spine
hide	describe	arrive	five	pipe	bite	realize
lime	outside	alive	mike	smile	stripe	surprise
site	provide	file	slide	slime	write	organise

igh					
right	tight	bright	tonight	higher	frighten
light	sightsee	might	flashlight	sigh	

Long /i/ Sound Words Cont'd

y					
shy	sky	reply	cyclone	nearby	why
by	spy	deny	magnify	myself	cry
dry	apply	try	butterfly	satisfy	July

y_e				
type	thyme	rhyme	paralyze	style
enzyme	hairstyle	analyze	byte	

ie					
tie	die	lie	untie	pie	tried

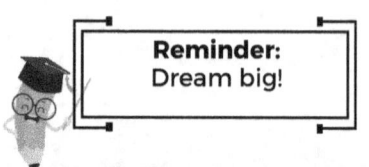

Reminder:
Dream big!

GRAPHEME & PHONEME CHARTING

Instruction: Listen to the word that the teacher calls.

Example: The word is **tidy.**

Tap out the sounds with your fingers

1 2 3 4

Say the Word	Tap out the sounds that you hear in the word				
Map the Sound Sound out the word and put a tick in the box for every sound that you hear	✓	✓	✓	✓	
Graph the Word Write the letter for each sound that you hear to spell the word. Write one sound in each box.	/t/	/i/	/d/	/y/	
Write out the whole word	tidy				

Grapheme & Phoneme Charting Cont'd

instruction: Listen to the word that the teacher calls.

Say the Word	Tap out the sounds that you hear in the word				
Map the Sound Sound out the word and put a tick in the box for every sound that you hear					
Graph the Word Write the letter for each sound that you hear to spell the word. Write one sound in each box.					
Write out the whole word					

Grapheme & Phoneme Charting Cont'd

Instruction: Listen to the word that the teacher calls.

Say the Word	Tap out the sounds that you hear in the word				
Map the Sound Sound out the word and put a tick in the box for every sound that you hear					
Graph the Word Write the letter for each sound that you hear to spell the word. Write one sound in each box.					
Write out the whole word					

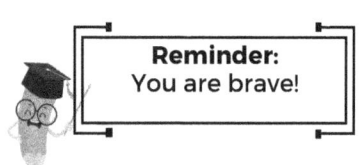

Reminder: You are brave!

WORD RECOGNITION

Mixed Word Recognition Activity
Long i Sound

idol ☐	die ☐	myself ☐	time ☐
item ☐	time ☐	high ☐	why ☐
bright ☐	thyme ☐	try ☐	style ☐
sky ☐	bicycle ☐	spider ☐	might ☐
pilot ☐	light ☐	library ☐	cry ☐
hydrant ☐	untie ☐	final ☐	silent ☐
fine ☐	nearby ☐		
kind ☐	cyclone ☐		

TOTAL: **TOTAL:**   **TOTAL:**   **TOTAL:**

Reminder:
You are clever!

Long /i/ Sound Reading Passage

The Kite

The kite flies high in the sky. It likes to glide above the bright, wide field. The sun shines, and the kite feels the wind lift it up. It can see the white clouds and tiny birds flying by. The kite's string is tied tight, so it won't fall. It is happy to fly and play all day long.

Number of long i sound words from the passage: _ _ _ _ _ _ _ _ _ _ _

Long /i/ Sound Reading Passage

The Life Cycle of the Butterflies

Butterflies have an amazing life cycle. They start as tiny eggs laid on leaves. After a while, the eggs hatch, and a small caterpillar comes out. The caterpillar eats and grows until it's ready to change. It wraps itself in a chrysalis, where it stays for some time. Inside, the caterpillar transforms into a butterfly. When it's time, the butterfly breaks free and spreads its wings to fly high in the sky. This journey from caterpillar to butterfly is called metamorphosis.

Number of long /i/ sound words from the passage: _ _ _ _ _ _ _ _ _

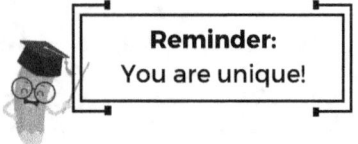

Reminder:
You are unique!

Long /i/ Reading Passage

The Science of Flight

The science of flight is fascinating. Airplanes, for instance, rely on principles like lift, thrust, and gravity to soar through the sky. Lift is created by the design of the wings, which are curved on top and flatter on the bottom. This shape forces the air to move faster above the wing and slower below, creating an upward force. Meanwhile, the engine provides the thrust needed to move forward, while gravity pulls the plane downward. Pilots must carefully balance these forces to maintain a steady flight. Mastering the skill of flying requires both knowledge and practice, making it a complex and exciting field.

Number of long /i/ sound words from the passage: _ _ _ _ _ _ _ _ _ _ _

Long /o/ Sound Words

o					
over	so	pony	focus	piano	potato
yogurt	locate	total	omit	moment	coma
banjo	rosy	donut	bonus		

oa					
oat	foam	boat	coal	road	charcoal
cocoa	throat	oak	groan	soak	loan
coach	moan	goat	soap	toast	

o_e					
stove	home	close	stove	spoke	telescope
stone	rope	nose	compose	remote	telephone
alone	hose	explode	suppose	tadpole	envelope

Long /o/ Sound Words Cont'd

OW				
bow	tow	glow	known	owner
row	yellow	low	shadow	fellow
throw	below	meadow	swallow	arrow
lower	window	blown	tomorrow	pillow
shown	narrow	grow	sparrow	blow

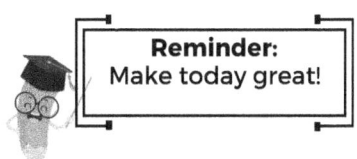

Reminder:
Make today great!

GRAPHEME & PHONEME CHARTING

Instruction: Listen to the word that the teacher calls.

Example: The word is blow.
Tap out the sounds with your fingers **1 2 3**

Say the Word	Tap out the sounds that you hear in the word				
Map the Sound Sound out the word and put a tick in the box for every sound that you hear	✓	✓	✓		
Graph the Word Write the letter for each sound that you hear to spell the word. Write one sound in each box.	/b/	/l/	/ow/		
Write out the whole word	blow				

Grapheme & Phoneme Charting Cont'd

Instruction: Listen to the word that the teacher calls.

Say the Word	Tap out the sounds that you hear in the word				
Map the Sound Sound out the word and put a tick in the box for every sound that you hear					
Graph the Word Write the letter for each sound that you hear to spell the word. Write one sound in each box.					
Write out the whole word					

Grapheme & Phoneme Charting Cont'd

Instruction: Listen to the word that the teacher calls.

Say the Word	Tap out the sounds that you hear in the word				
Map the Sound Sound out the word and put a tick in the box for every sound that you hear					
Graph the Word Write the letter for each sound that you hear to spell the word. Write one sound in each box.					
Write out the whole word					

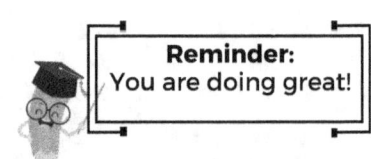

Reminder: You are doing great!

WORD RECOGNITION

Mixed Word Recognition Activity
Long o Sound

boat ☐	focus ☐	omit ☐	compose ☐
grow ☐	tomato ☐	total ☐	sow ☐
toe ☐	hallow ☐	bonus ☐	goat ☐
hole ☐	hello ☐	coach ☐	throat ☐
goal ☐	brow ☐	oats ☐	wrote ☐
halo ☐	coast ☐	stole ☐	mold ☐

| TOTAL: | TOTAL: | TOTAL: | TOTAL: |

Spelling By Pattern

Instruction: Use the shapes and patterns provided to spell each word in the box below.

boat   know   shallow   pony   phone   focus

telephone   toe   toad   explode   soap   hoe

Long /o/ Sound Reading Passage

Boats

Boats float on the ocean. They move slowly across the blue waves. Sometimes, a big boat carries lots of people and cargo. Other times, a small boat might just have a few folks on board. The sun shines brightly on the water, making it sparkle. Seagulls fly overhead, and you can hear their calls. Boating is a fun way to enjoy a day on the sea.

Number of long o sound words from the passage: _ _ _ _ _ _ _ _ _ _ _

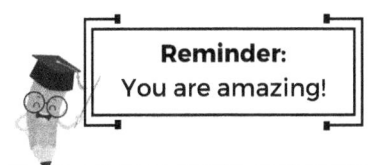

Reminder:
You are amazing!

Long /o/ Sound Reading Passage

The Role of Volcanoes

Volcanoes play a crucial role in Earth's geology. When a volcano erupts, it releases molten rock, known as lava, from beneath the Earth's crust. This lava cools and solidifies, forming new land. The eruptions can also release gases and ash into the atmosphere. Over time, the layers of lava build up, creating a cone-shaped mountain. These volcanoes can create fertile soil around them, which helps plants grow.

Despite their potential for destruction, volcanoes are important for shaping the landscape and enriching the environment.

Number of long o sound words from the passage: _ _ _ _ _ _ _ _ _

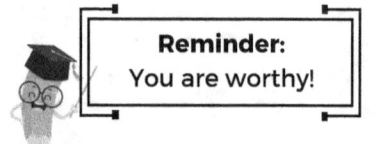

Reminder:
You are worthy!

Long /o/ Reading Passage

The Ocean

The ocean is home to a diverse range of creatures and ecosystems. One fascinating group of animals found in the ocean is the dolphin. Dolphins are known for their playful behavior and high intelligence. They use echo-location to find food and navigate through the water. The ocean also has vast coral reefs, which provide shelter and food for many fish and marine species. Coral reefs are sometimes called the "rainforests of the sea" because of their incredible biodiversity. Additionally, the deep ocean floor is home to unique organisms that thrive in the dark, cold depths. Exploring the ocean reveals new and amazing life forms every day.

Number of long o sound words from the passage: _ _ _ _ _ _ _ _ _ _

Long /u/ Sound Words

u				
human	occupy	humour	unit	futile
universe	fuel	evaluate	humid	usual
future	pupil	uniform	mutual	cupid

ue				
rescue	value	blue	cue	statue
miscue	barbeque	true	due	eulogy
continue	pursue	argue	tissue	clue
subdue	venue	hue	issue	

u_e				
custume	cube	use	mute	confuse
assume	huge	abuse	allure	produce
fumes	tune	fuse	minute	

Long /u/ Sound Words Cont'd

ew					
new	mildew	renew	knew	interview	

WORD RECOGNITION

Mixed Word Recognition Activity
Long u sounds

Tuesday ☐	tune ☐	statue ☐
unity ☐	actual ☐	mildew ☐
use ☐	solution ☐	cupid ☐
argue ☐	reduce ☐	humid ☐
utility ☐	duke ☐	cube ☐
unicorn ☐	gratitude ☐	duly ☐
pursue ☐	tube ☐	duty ☐

TOTAL:	TOTAL:	TOTAL:

Reminder:
Trust the process!

Word Recognition Activity

Instruction: Listen to the teacher and **colour** the word that you hear.

usual	fuse	united	argue	cube	molecule
unit	futile	union	rescue	immune	genuine
menu	review	unique	excuse	diffuse	tribute
curfew	fued	pursue	continue	nephew	eucalyptus

Spelling By Pattern

Instruction: Use the shapes and patterns provided to spell each word in the box below.

news   mute   statue   tutor   cupid   unity

mutual   flute   stew   use   mildew   dew

Long /u/ Sound Reading Passage

<u>Jingles</u>

Hug a mule, sing a tune,
Under the sky, see the moon!
Blue birds fly, kangaroos hop,
Long u sounds, we won't stop!

The sky is blue, the flowers grew,
A cute mule says, "How do you do?"
A new tune plays, so sweet and true,
Let's sing along, just me and you!

Number of long u sound words from the passage: _ _ _ _ _ _ _ _ _

Long /u/ Sound Reading Passage

The Moon

The moon is Earth's closest neighbour in space, and it has a huge impact on our planet. One interesting fact about the moon is that it doesn't produce its own light. Instead, it reflects the light of the sun. The moon goes through different phases as it orbits Earth. Sometimes, we see a full moon, which looks bright and round. At other times, we only see a small part of the moon, known as a crescent. These phases continue in a cycle, repeating every month. The moon also affects the ocean's tides, pulling the water towards it and creating high and low tides.

Number of long u sound words from the passage: _ _ _ _ _ _ _ _ _ _

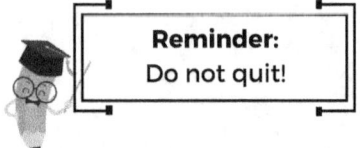

Reminder:
Do not quit!

Long /u/ Reading Passage

The Value of Renewable Energy

Renewable energy is crucial for the future of our planet. Unlike fossil fuels, renewable sources like solar, wind, and hydropower do not deplete natural resources. Solar panels, for example, capture energy from the sun and convert it into electricity. Wind turbines use the power of the wind to generate energy without producing pollution. Hydropower utilizes the force of moving water to produce clean energy. By investing in renewable energy, we reduce our reliance on fossil fuels and help protect the environment. It's essential that we continue to pursue new and innovative ways to use these sustainable resources.

Number of long u sound words from the passage: _ _ _ _ _ _ _ _ _ _ _ _

TYPES OF SYLLABLES

There are seven types of syllables. The acronym **CLOVER D** is used to remember them.

Type	Example
C = **C**losed Syllable	**"hot"**
L = Consonant **–le**	"han-**dle**"
O = **O**pen Syllable	"**pa**-per"
V = **V**owel Combinations	"**ea**t"
E = Silent **E** rule (v_e)	**"ma̲de"**
R = **R-Controlled** Vowels	"h**ur**t," "b**ar**," "sh**ir**t," "f**or**," "h**er**"
D = **D**ipthong	"t**oo**th"

Closed	A syllable in which a single vowel is followed by a consonant. The vowel is usually short.	v̆ c	cat rab/bit nap/kin
Consonant –le	An unaccented final syllable containing a consonant and -le.	c l e	bub/ble sta/ple cir/cle
Open	A syllable ending with a single vowel. The vowel is usually long.	v̄	ti/ger ba/by pa/per
Vowel Team	A syllable containing two letters that together make one vowel sound.	v̄ v́	team float seed
Silent E	A syllable with the long vowel-consonant- silent e pattern.	v̄ c é	bake pine bone
R-Controlled	A syllable in which the vowel(s) is followed by the single letter. The vowel sound is "controlled" by the r.	v r	car board fort
D = Dipthong	A syllable containing two vowels in which a new vowel sound is formed by the combination of both vowel sounds.	v v	boil cloud look

Closed Syllable

What is a Closed Syllable?

A closed syllable is a type of syllable in a word where the syllable ends with a consonant. This means that the vowel in the syllable is followed by one or more consonants, and it typically makes a short vowel sound.

Example Words with Closed Syllables:

- cat: The syllable "cat" ends with the consonant "t," so it's a closed syllable.
- lemon: There are two closed syllables in this word. The syllable "lem" ends with the consonant "m" and the syllable "on" ends with the consonant "n" making them closed syllables.
- punishment: There are three closed syllables in this word. The syllable "pun" ends with "n", "ish" ends with "sh" and "ment" ends with "t".

Highlights:

- A closed syllable ends in a consonant.
- The vowel sound in a closed syllable is usually short.
- Most one-syllable words with a single vowel followed by a consonant are closed syllables (e.g., "hat," "red," "sit").

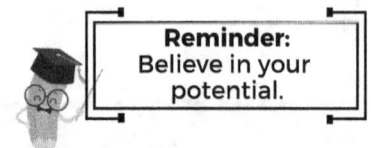

Reminder:
Believe in your potential.

Activity:

Instruction: Colour the closed syllable words in the clouds below.

to	she	chat	be
top	free	fly	gym
lend	kiss	trip	ring
why	drink	go	hi
try	do	turn	me

Instructions: Break the words into syllables using a slash.
Decide if the **first** syllable is closed.
Tick the box if it is a closed syllable.

e.g.	napkin	nap/kin	✓
	acorn		☐
	milo		☐
	baby		☐
	pocket		☐
	candy		☐
	cargo		☐
	simple		☐
	razor		☐
	pilot		☐
	unpack		☐
	crazy		☐

paper		☐
mention		☐
hero		☐
jacket		☐
kitten		☐
lion		☐
cocoa		☐
pumpkin		☐
lady		☐

Reminder:
Learn, grow,
and succeed.

Instruction: Put the following words in the correct column:

can	so	it	dog
cat	insect	absent	apron	rabbit	man
pen	subject	be	iron	go	submit
sudden	hotel	oven	do	velvet	she
basic	kitten	happen	bonus	music
mishap	relax	pupil	unit	even	pen

One Closed Syllable	One Open Syllable	Two Closed Syllables	Open & Closed Syllables

Consonant –le

What is a Consonant –le syllable?

A consonant-le syllable is a type of syllable that appears at the end of a word. It consists of a consonant followed by the letters "le." The consonant and the "le" together form the syllable.

Important Note

1. **Structure:** The syllable is made up of a consonant followed by "le" (e.g., "ble," "dle," "fle").
2. **Silent 'e':** The "e" in the "le" is silent, and the consonant + "le" together make a single syllable.
3. **Placement:** Consonant-le syllables always appear at the end of a word.

Examples of Consonant-le Syllables:

- **table:** The word "table" has two syllables. The second syllable "ble" is a consonant-le syllable.
- **apple:** The word "apple" has two syllables. The second syllable "ple" is a consonant-le syllable.
- **handle:** The word "handle" has two syllables. The second syllable "dle" is a consonant-le syllable.
- **puzzle:** The word "puzzle" has two syllables. The second syllable "zle" is a consonant-le syllable.

How to Divide Consonant-le Words into Syllables:

1. Find the consonant-le at the end of the word.
2. Count back three letters from the end of the word to divide the syllables.

Example:

- "candle" is divided into "can" / "dle"
- "rattle" is divided into "rat" / "tle"

Instruction: Divide the following words into syllables. Remember to Count back three letters from the end of the word to divide the syllables. Call the words for the teacher.

1. table _____ ☐
2. puzzle _____ ☐
3. cradle _____ ☐
4. cycle _____ ☐
5. uncle _____ ☐
6. bangle _____ ☐
7. mantle _____ ☐
8. bundle _____ ☐
9. ripple _____ ☐
10. buckle _____ ☐

Activity:

Instruction: Write the consonant + le words for each picture.
An Example is given.

 drizzle

 ____

 ____

 ____

 ____

 ____

 ____

 ____

 ____

Reminder:
Progress,
not perfection

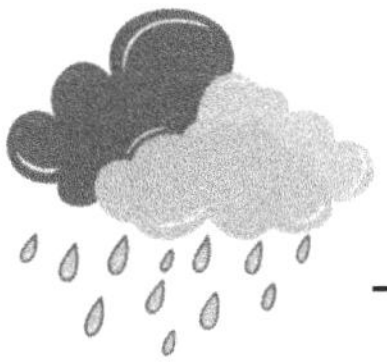

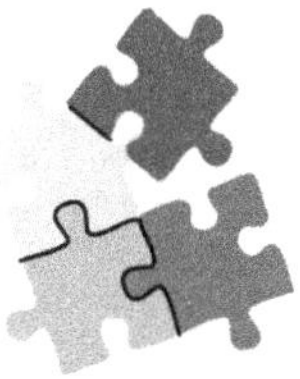

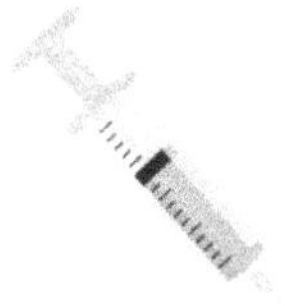

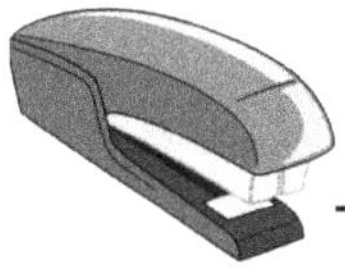

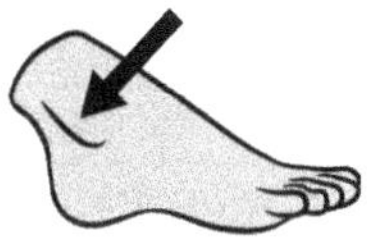

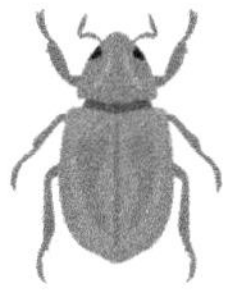

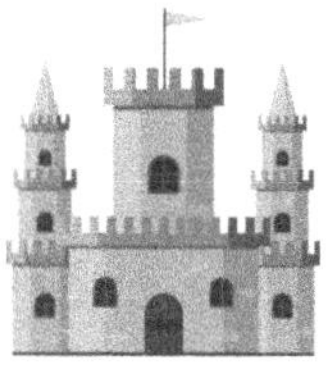

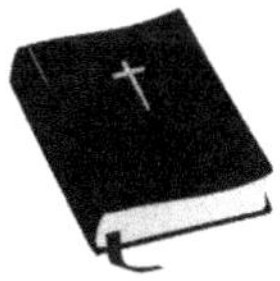

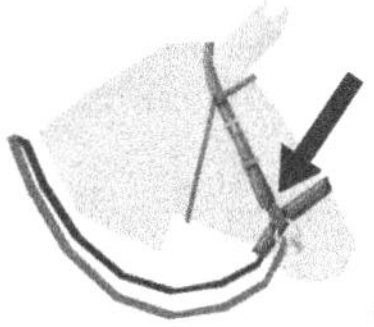

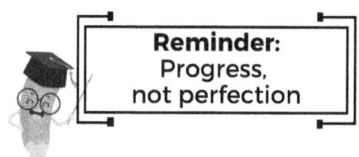

Open Syllable

 An open syllable is a type of syllable in which the vowel is at the end of the syllable, and it usually has a long vowel sound. Because the syllable ends with a vowel, the vowel is "open" and not followed by a consonant.

Important Note
- In an open syllable, the vowel is the last letter of the syllable. For example, in the word "he," the syllable ends with the vowel "e."
- The vowel in an open syllable usually makes its long sound (the sound it says when you recite the alphabet). For example, in the word "go," the "o" sounds like its name, "O."

One-Syllable Examples:
- "Me": The syllable "me" ends with the vowel "e," and it has a long "e" sound.
- "No": The syllable "no" ends with the vowel "o," and it has a long "o" sound.
- "Hi": The syllable "hi" ends with the vowel "i," and it has a long "i" sound.

Multi-Syllable Words with Open Syllables:
"ba/by": The first syllable "ba" is an open syllable, and the "a" has a long sound.
"va/ca/tion": The first two syllables are open, and the "a" gives a long sound.
"to/ma/to": All three syllables are open with the "o" and the "a" making a long sound.

- Not all vowels in open syllables make a long sound (e.g., "to" in "tomorrow" has a short sound). However, typically, open syllables feature long vowel sounds, especially in one-syllable words.

List of Open Syllable Words

Instruction: Break the words into syllables then call them. Highlight the open syllable parts.

One Syllable	Two Syllables	Three Syllables	Four Syllables
me	baby	tomato	macaroni
go	open	potato	radiator
no	tiger	idea	education
so	music	radio	photography
he	silent	video	calculator
me	moment	studio	scenario
go	robot	piano	
we	human	cameo	
hi	final	veto	
she	paper	patio	
be	zero		
by	ego		
my	pilot		
spy	hero		
shy			
fly			
try			
cry			
why			
sky			
fry			
by			

Activity:

Instruction: Read the words below and split the words into
syllables on the blanks.

1. final: _____

2. able: _____

3. began: _____

4. giant: _____

5. solution: _____

6. potato: _____

7. broken: _____

8. quiet: _____

9. hotel: _____

10. equip: _____

11. peanut: _____

12. crazy: _____

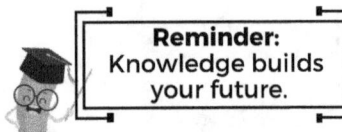

Activity:

Instruction: Colour the circle(s) to state whether the syllables are open or closed, open and closed, closed and open, open and open, closed and closed. The first one is done for you.

	OPEN	OPEN	CLOSED	CLOSED
fla/vour	○	●	●	○
bend	○	○	○	○
bro/ken	○	○	○	○
New/man	○	○	○	○
sky	○	○	○	○
men/u	○	○	○	○
en/ter	○	○	○	○
i/dol	○	○	○	○
fab/ric	○	○	○	○
mu/sic	○	○	○	○
ho/ri/zon	○	○	○	○

Vowel Consonant e (VCe)

The VCE pattern consists of a vowel followed by a consonant and an "e" at the end of the word (V-C-e). This pattern is sometimes called the "magic e" or "silent e" rule.

Examples: Some common examples include "cake," "home," "ride," and "note."

Key Points:

1. **The Silent 'e':**
   - The 'e' at the end of a word in the VCE pattern is silent; it does not make a sound.
   - Instead, its role is to change the sound of the preceding vowel.

1. **Vowel Sound Change:**
   - In a VCE word, the vowel before the consonant typically makes a long vowel sound.
   - A long vowel sound is when the vowel sounds like its name. For example:
     "a" in "cake" sounds like the letter "A."
     "o" in "home" sounds like the letter "O."

Exceptions:
   - There are some exceptions to the VCE rule, such as the word "have," where the 'e' does not make the preceding vowel long.

Activity:

Instruction: Call the short vowel sound words in the left column, then add the silent e at the end in the right column. Now call the words that you have made.

at	at _____
ut	ut _____
et	et _____
ot	ot _____
it	it _____

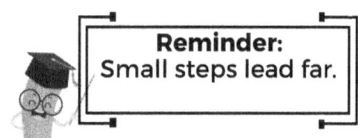

Reminder:
Small steps lead far.

Activity:

Instruction: Add e to the end of each word to make a new word.

bat____   plum____

cut____   sin____

kit____   spin____

trip____   cub____

rot____   van____

met____   cod____

fat____   hug____

not____   cloth____

ton____   bath____

slim____   her____

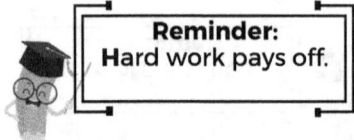

A_E Words

One-Syllable A-E Words	Two-Syllable A-E Words
cake	pirate
grate	relate
late	remake
plane	debate
brave	inflate
scrape	parade
gate	mistake
rate	update
slate	escape

E_E Words

One-Syllable E-E Words	Two-Syllable E-E Words
Eve	extreme
these	serene
Steve	complete
gene	intervene
theme	concrete

I_E Words

One-Syllable I-E Words	Two-Syllable I-E Words
like	invite
time	inspire
write	decide
drive	ignite
shine	survive
bite	recite
slide	provide
hide	excite

O_E Words

One-Syllable O-E Words	Two-Syllable O-E Words
rote	promote
home	remote
node	explode
bone	devote
phone	propose
pose	envelope
alone	compose
close	suppose

U_E Words

One-Syllable U-E Words	Two-Syllable U-E Words
mute	amuse
use	excuse
cube	profuse
rule	refuse
June	consume
prune	include
tube	reduce
flute	compute

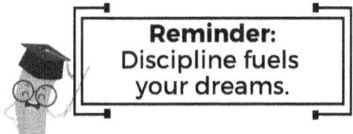

Reminder:
Discipline fuels
your dreams.

Mixed VCE Word Recognition

Call the following words for your teacher. Put a tick in the box if the answer is correct or an X if the answer is incorrect.

note ☐	connote ☐	concrete ☐
cone ☐	stone ☐	reduce ☐
blame ☐	huge ☐	drone ☐
vote ☐	kite ☐	provide ☐
late ☐	like ☐	survive ☐
salute ☐	phone ☐	escape ☐
complete ☐	state ☐	envelope ☐
delete ☐	shake ☐	amuse ☐

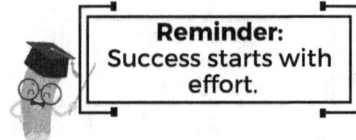

VCE Reading Passage

A Nice Ride Home

Kate has a bike. She likes to ride it down the wide lane by her home. One day, she rode her bike far away. She saw a big white gate. She went inside and saw a huge cake on a plate! Kate smiled and took a bite. "Yum!" she said. But then, it was late. Kate rode back home, fast and safe. Her mom said, "You are brave, Kate!"

VCE Reading Passage

The Life of a Whale

Whales are the largest animals on Earth. These huge creatures live in the ocean, where they swim gracefully through the waves. A whale's size is incredible—some can be as long as two school buses!

One interesting fact about whales is that they breathe air, just like people. Whales rise to the surface of the water to take a breath. They have a special hole on top of their heads called a blowhole. When they exhale, water sprays into the air like a fountain.

Whales have a strong sense of hearing. They use sound to communicate with each other, even from miles away. This ability to make and hear sounds helps them find food, navigate the ocean, and stay in touch with their family.

Whales are gentle giants. Even though they are big, they eat tiny creatures called krill. They take a huge gulp of water, then push the water out while trapping the krill inside their mouths. These amazing animals have long lives. Some whales can live up to 80 years or more! Whales are important to the ocean and must be protected to continue to thrive in the sea.

Activity:

Instruction: Read the following sentences aloud.

1. Jake will bake a cake for his sister's birthday.

2. The lake was calm and reflected the clear blue sky.

3. She used a rake to gather the leaves in the yard.

4. Mike decided to ride his bike to the store.

5. The snake slid into its cave to hide from the sun.

6. Please close the door gently so it doesn't make noise.

7. The flame of the candle flickered in the breeze.

8. He was excited to vote for the first time.

9. The mule helped carry supplies up the mountain.

10. She wore a white dress to the event.

Spelling By Pattern

Instructions: Write the words in their correct pattern.

abide   plate   flute   unite   hate   spite

these   use   bathe   close   theme   pose

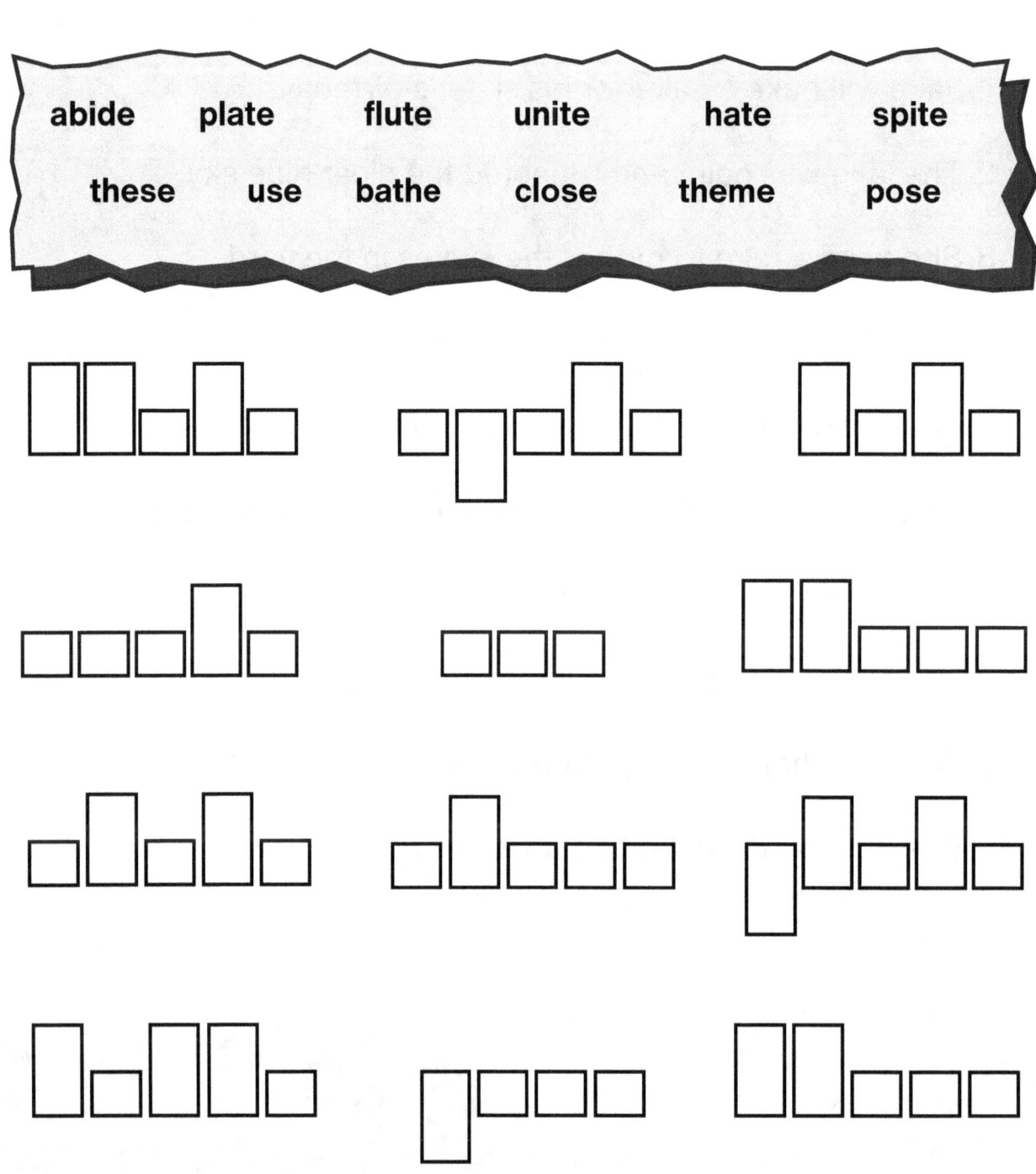

Vowel Team Syllables

A vowel team syllable is a type of syllable in which two or more vowels work together to make a single vowel sound. These combinations can represent long, short, or diphthong vowel sounds.

Examples of Vowel Teams:

- Long Vowel Sounds:

    "ea" as in "team" – Makes the long "e" sound.

    "ai" as in "rain" – Makes the long "a" sound.

    "oa" as in "boat" – Makes the long "o" sound.

    "ee" as in "see" – Makes the long "e" sound.

- Diphthong Sounds:

    "oi" as in "boil" – Makes an "oy" sound.

    "ou" as in "out" – Makes an "ow" sound.

    "au" as in "author" – Makes an "aw" sound.

- Other Sounds:

    "oo" as in "book" – Can make a short "u" sound or a long "oo" sound as in "moon."

Features of Vowel Teams:

- Vowel teams often make the vowel sound longer or change it altogether.
- These teams can consist of two, three, or even four vowels working together to produce a single sound.
- Vowel team syllables are usually pronounced with a smooth, blended sound, rather than breaking the vowels into separate sounds.

Vowel Team Syllables Cont'd

Rules of Thumb:

1. Long vowel sound: When two vowels go walking, the first one usually does the talking (as in "rain" or "team").
2. Diphthongs: These vowel teams create a gliding sound within the same syllable (as in "boil" or "cloud").

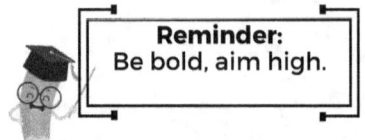

Reminder:
Be bold, aim high.

Vowel Team Syllables—The Long ā Sound

Remember: When two vowels go walking, the first one does the talking and calls its name. Try to call the words below.

AI Words	AY Word
aim	bay
aid	day
air	lay
bail	tray
main	stay
laid	delay
grail	midday
sprain	relay
afraid	Monday
refrain	holiday
train	array
ailment	may
sailboat	today
chain	clay
gain	pray
trait	play
straight	bay
airport	hay
frail	quay
praise	bray

Activity:

Instruction: Read these sentences with vowel teams, "ai" and "ay". .

1. The **rain** poured heavily on the **main** street.

2. The **train** arrived at the station right on time.

3. She used a **paint**brush to create a beautiful **sailboat** painting.

4. The **snail** moved slowly across the wet **trail**.

5. He hoped to **gain** some insight from the **pain** he endured.

6. They decided to take a short **day** trip to the **bay**.

7. The **gray** sky indicated that it might **rain** later.

8. The children love to **play** in the **hay** during the summer.

9. The **mail** was delivered early on a sunny **day**.

10. She braided her **hair** while sitting on the porch in the **midday** sun.

Vowel Team Syllables—The Long ē Sound.

Remember: When two vowels go walking the first one does the talking. "ei" "ea" "ey" "ee".

EI Words	EA Words	EY Words	EE Words
either	please	key	seed
neither	eat	monkey	feed
seize	eagle	donkey	breed
forfeit	beach	turkey	need
protein	reach	honey	speed
deceive	steal	chimney	meet
being	peach	parsley	keep
weird	bean	money	kneel
heirs	lean	valley	been
their	easy		heel
leisure	leak		steel
ceiling	increase		seem
receipt	seat		queen
caffeine	tease		speech
	least		freeze
	preach		three
	scream		eel
	dream		needle

Activity:

Instruction: Read the following sentences with the long ē sound.

1. The **eagle** soared high above the **sea.**

2. He tried to **conceive** a plan to solve the difficult problem

3. The **sheep** grazed **peacefully** in the meadow.

4. The **teacher** asked the class to be quiet during the test.

5. They watched the sunset turn the sky a soft **peachy** colour.

6. She wore a **beaded** necklace with a **beautiful** dress.

7. The **ceiling** of the room was painted **cream.**

8. The **monkey** swung from **tree** to tree with **ease.**

9. The **hockey** game ended with the home team taking the **lead.**

10. The thief tried to **seize** the **money** and escape quickly.

Spelling By Pattern

Instruction: Write the words in their correct pattern.

key   either   cream   breed   please   valley

needle   speed   chimney   caffeine   increase   meal

Vowel Team Syllables—The Long ō Sound

Remember: When two vowels go walking the first one does the talking. "oa" "oe"

OA Words	OE Words
boat	woe
goat	doe
float	aloe
road	tiptoe
cloak	oboe
coach	woe
approach	hoe
moat	roe
groan	foe
soap	
oats	
croak	
throat	
encroach	
loaf	
toad	
roast	

<u>Spelling on the Stairs</u>

Instruction: Listen to the word that the teacher calls. Spell the word step by step.

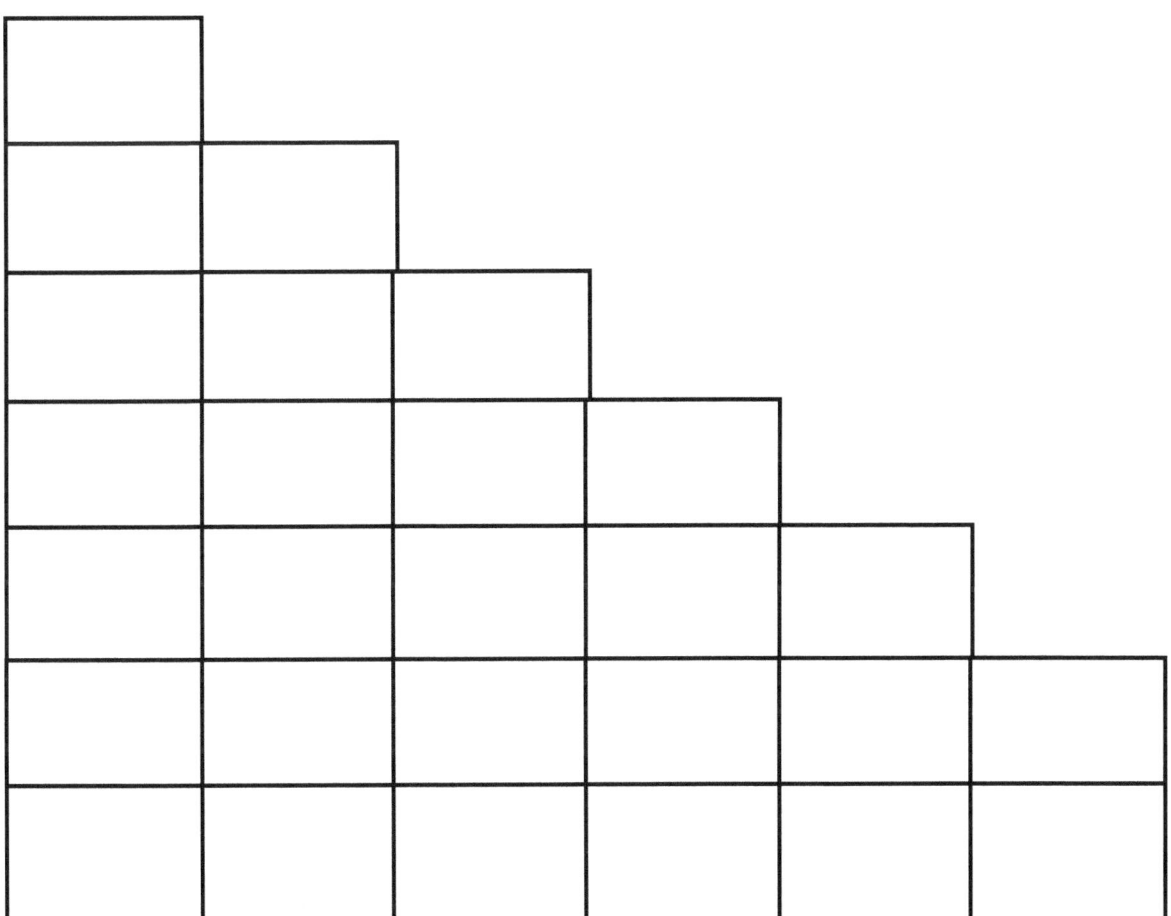

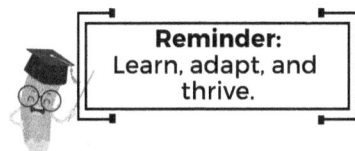

<u>Spelling on the Stairs</u>

Instruction: Listen to the word that the teacher calls. Spell the word step by step.

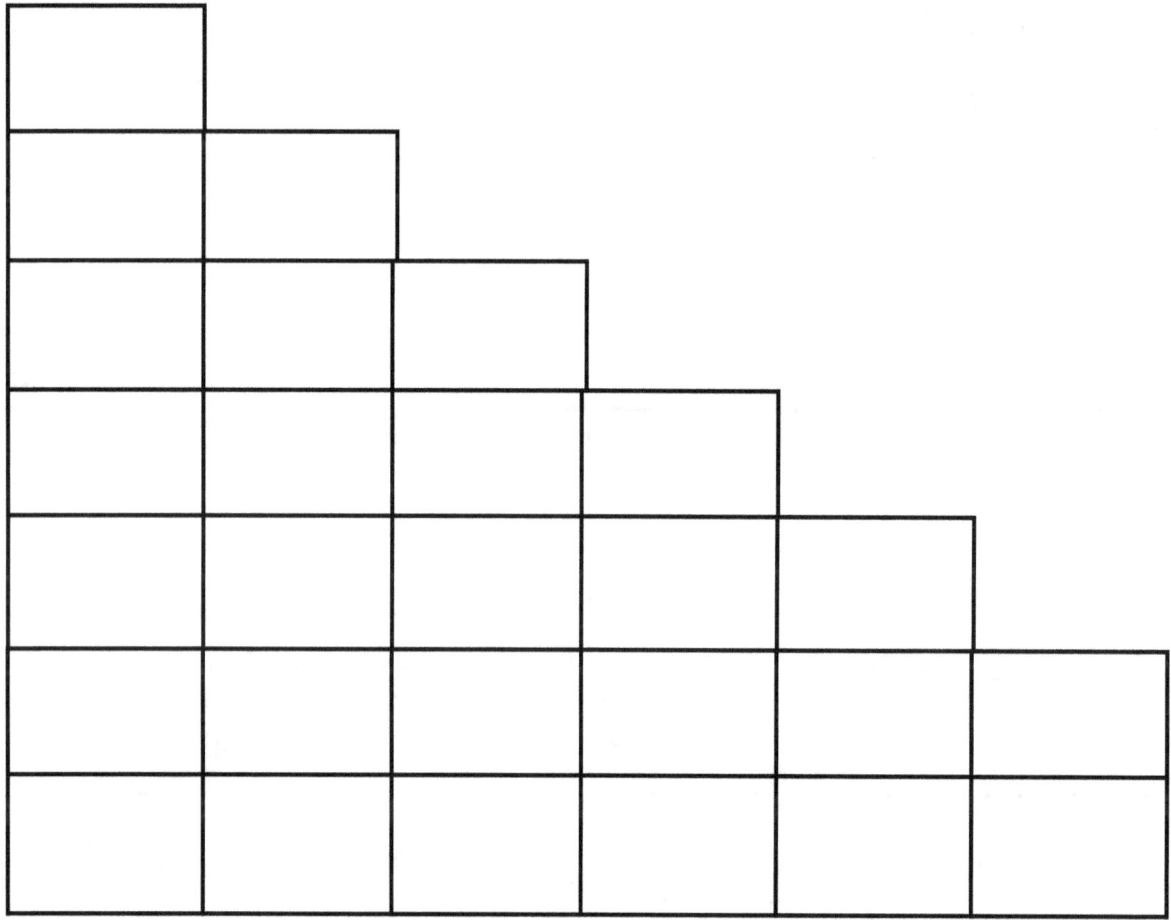

<u>Spelling on the Stairs</u>

Instruction: Listen to the word that the teacher calls. Spell the word step by step.

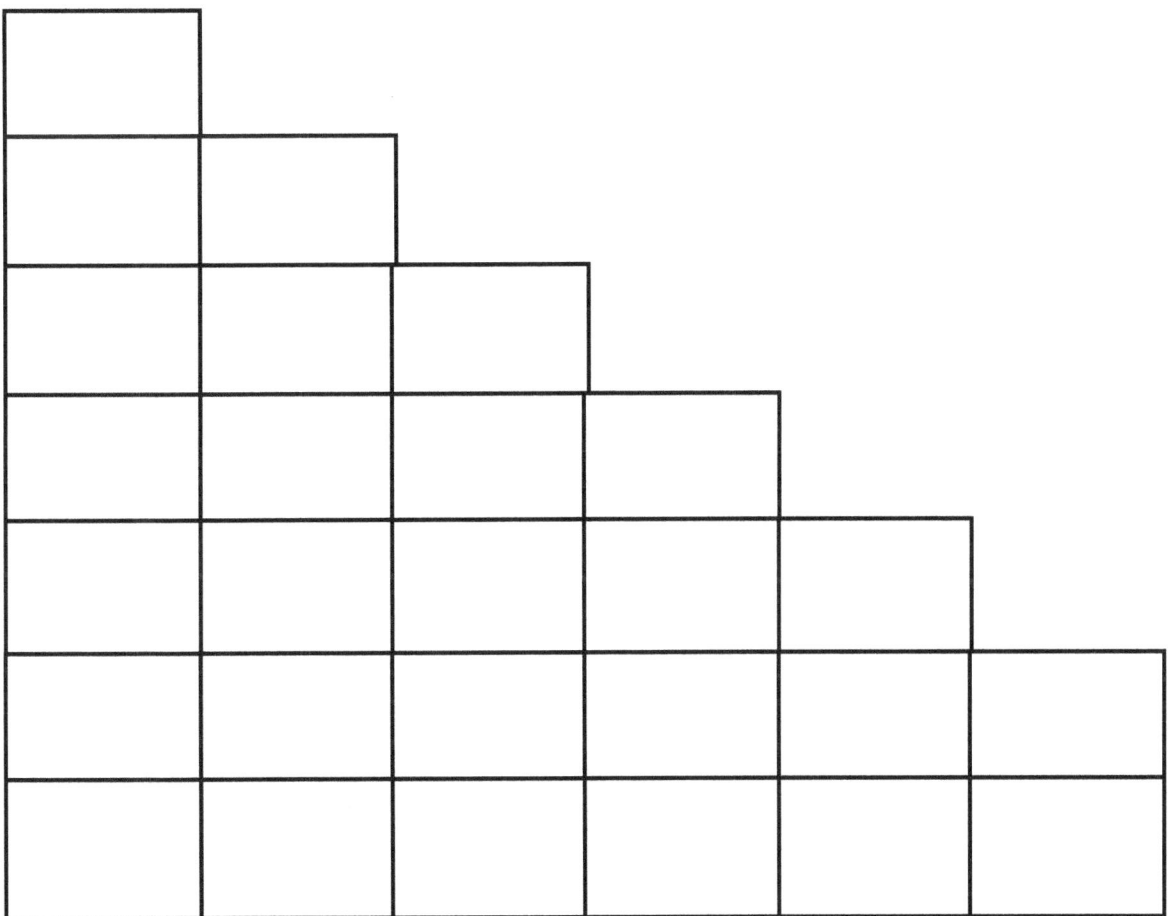

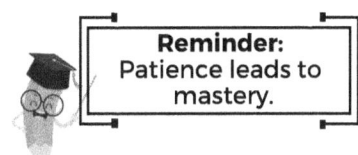

Diphthongs

Another name for diphthongs is 'gliding vowels.' These are phonemes, or sounds, that contain two different vowel sounds within the same syllable. This means that when you pronounce a diphthong, you produce two distinct sounds.

AW
hawk, bawl
straw, awful
flaw, saw

AU
haul, cause
caught, author
pauper, fault

EW
stew, cashew
blew, chew
few, new

OO
tooth, root
bamboo, soon
room, food

OW
owl, brown
flower, growl
howl, bow

OU
loud, found
couch, round
out, cloud

OI
coin, point
noise, choice
toil, spoil, oil

OY
boy, employ
enjoy, oyster
decoy, toy

Activity:

Instruction: Use the correct diphthong (ow, au, oo, oi) to complete the words:

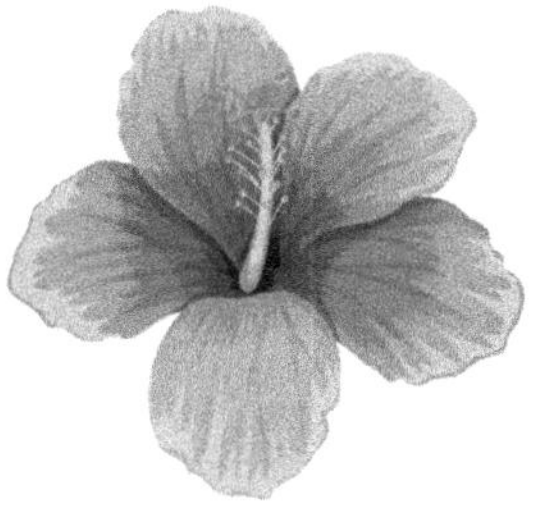

fl ___ ___ er	l ___ ___ gh
c ___ ___ n	cl ___ ___ n
n ___ ___ se	t ___ ___ th

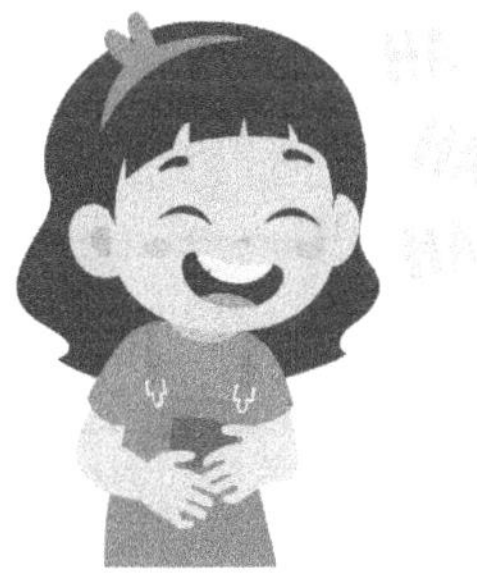

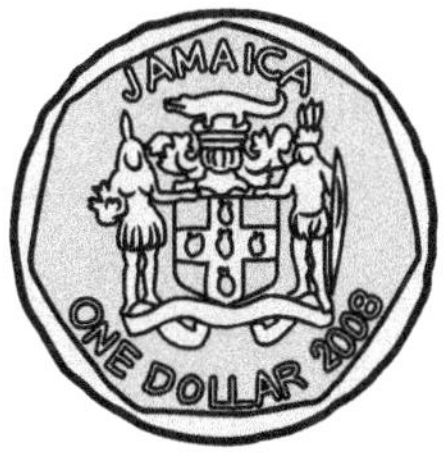

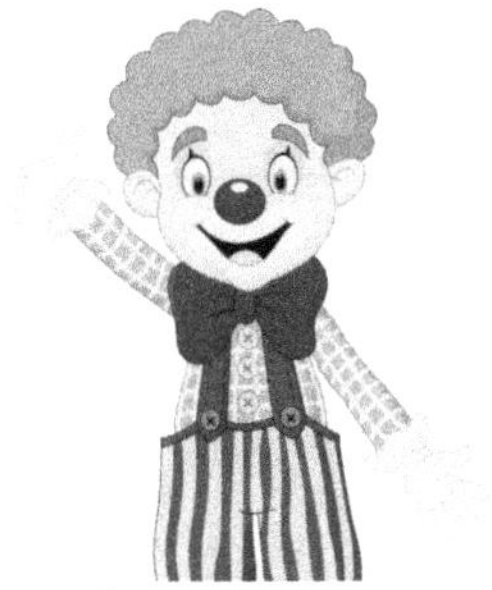

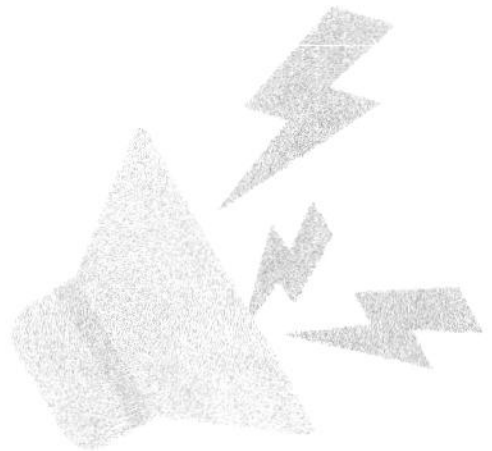

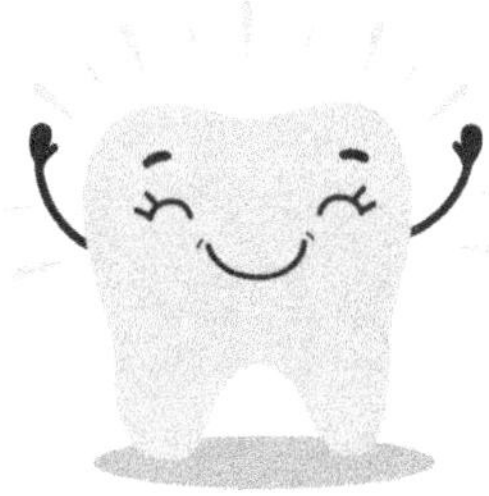

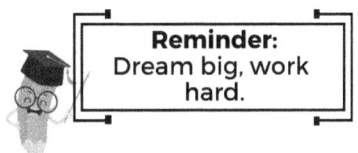

Activity:

Instruction: Create three words using the given diphthongs:

1. aw: _____ _____ _____

2. au: _____ _____ _____

3. ew: _____ _____ _____

4. oo: _____ _____ _____

5. oi: _____ _____ _____

6. oy: _____ _____ _____

Activity:

Instruction: Write a sentence for each word:

1. claw

   ....

2. caught

   ....

3. stew

   ....

4. moon

   ....

5. coin

   ....

6. toy

   ....

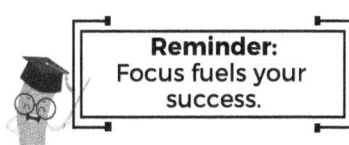

Reminder:
Focus fuels your success.

R Controlled Vowels

 R-controlled vowels, also known as "bossy R" vowels, occur when a vowel is followed by the letter "r". This changes the way the vowel sounds. Instead of the vowel making its usual short or long sound, it is controlled by the "r," resulting in a unique or special sound.

There are three R-controlled vowel sounds. They are as follows:

1. **–ar** says **r.** That is, it calls the name of the letter **r** as in "far"
2. **-or** says "or" as in "for".
3. **-er, -ir,** and **–ur** say **/r/.** That is, they all make the sound of "r" as in "fir," "her," and "curl."

Words with r-controlled vowels can be tricky to spell because the sounds are often similar, making it difficult to distinguish between "er," "ir," and "ur." One solution is to practice these words as sight words. The more you see these words the better your chance of spelling them correctly.

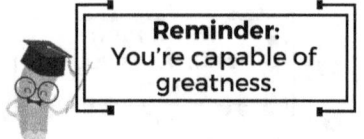

Reminder:
You're capable of greatness.

Activity:

Instruction: Practice calling the following words. Remember the sounds of the R-controlled vowels.

AR Words	OR Words	IR Words	ER Words	UR Words
star	form	third	germs	blur
ardent	cord	stir	certify	burp
hard	storm	fir	cover	curse
scarf	lord	bird	nerve	turn
farm	stork	first	verb	murder
dwarf	corn	chirp	letter	nurse
art	for	first	water	lurk
barn	store	dirt	after	purge
spark	floor	girl	answer	purple
charm	dorm	firm	nerd	turkey
margin	support	birthday	were	curl
lark	gorge	shirt	vertical	turtle
quart	torch	Irving	nerve	surge
harp	world	girt		jury
smart	port	circumstance		hurt

Activity:

Instruction: Write at least 5 more words in each column.
Be prepared to call them.

AR Words	OR Words	ER Words	IR Words	UR Words

Activity:

Instruction: The following words are **mixed R-controlled words.**
Call them and the teacher will **tick** them off if they are correct.

murder ☐	first ☐	twirl ☐
story ☐	curl ☐	murk ☐
hurry ☐	swirl ☐	flirt ☐
cord ☐	sport ☐	pervert ☐
birth ☐	large ☐	girl ☐
artist ☐	spark ☐	harm ☐
chirp ☐	worth ☐	dart ☐
burden ☐	perch ☐	argument ☐
north ☐	hurt ☐	torn ☐
	dirty ☐	

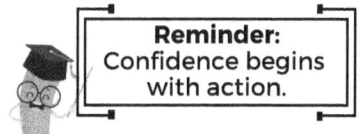

Reminder:
Confidence begins
with action.

Reading Passage Activity

The World of Sharks

Sharks are fascinating creatures. These powerful predators play a vital role in maintaining the balance of marine ecosystems.

There are over 500 different species of sharks, ranging from the tiny dwarf lantern shark, which is only about six inches long, to the enormous whale shark, which can grow up to 40 feet in length.

Sharks have a unique body structure that helps them survive in their aquatic environment. Their skeletons are made of cartilage, which is lighter than bone, allowing them to move quickly through the water. Sharks also have several rows of sharp teeth that they use to catch and eat their prey. If a shark loses a tooth, a new one will quickly replace it.

One of the most remarkable features of sharks is their ability to sense electrical fields in the water. This ability helps them locate prey even in complete darkness or murky waters. Sharks also have an excellent sense of smell, which they use to detect even the faintest scent of blood from miles away.

Despite their fearsome reputation, most sharks are not dangerous to humans. In fact, sharks are often more at risk from humans than we are from them. Many shark species are threatened by overfishing and habitat loss, making conservation efforts crucial for their survival.

Sharks are an essential part of the ocean's ecosystem, and protecting them is important for maintaining the health of our oceans. By learning more about these incredible animals, we can help ensure that they continue to thrive in the wild for generations to come.

Questions:

1). How many species of sharks are there?

_____

2). What material makes up a shark's skeleton?

_____

3). How do sharks replace lost teeth?

_____

4). What special ability helps sharks locate prey in the dark?

_____

5). Why are conservation efforts important for sharks?

_____

CONSONANT DIGRAPHS

 Consonant digraphs are pairs of consonants that unite to create one sound. That sound is different from the sound each letter would make on its own. The two letters work as a team in a digraph to produce a unique pronunciation.

Some common examples of consonant digraphs are:

- "ch" – The letters "c" and "h" when combined can create three sounds. They are "ch" as is chair, "sh" as in chef, and "k" as in character

- "sh" as in "sheet" – The letters "s" and "h" combine to create the "sh" sound.

- "th" as in "thin" or "this" – The letters "t" and "h" can create either a soft "th" sound as in "thin" or a harder "th" sound as in "this."

- "wh" as in "whale" – The letters "w" and "h" create the "wh" sound, though in some accents, this may be pronounced as just a "w" sound.

- "ph" as in "phone" – The letters "p" and "h" create an "f" sound.

- "ck" as in "back" – The letters "c" and "k" combine to produce a single "k" sound.

- "qu" as in "queen" – The letters "q" and "u" combine to make a single /kw/ sound
- "mb" as in "comb" – The letters "m" and "b" are combined but only the "m" is pronounced. The "b" is silent
- "kn" as in "know" –The letters "k" and "n" are combined but the "k" is silent and the "n" is pronounced.
- "ng" as in "sing" – "ng" digraph produces a nasal sound.

Activity:

Instruction: Write at least ten words in each column for each digraph. Be prepared to call the words for your teacher.

kn	ck	ch	ng	wh

qu	th	mb	ph	sh

Reading Passage Activity

Alligators-Ancient Hunters

Alligators are strong animals that live in swamps, rivers, and lakes. They have thick, tough skin that helps protect them from danger. Alligators are known for their sharp teeth, which they use to catch fish, birds, and other small animals. When they need to rest, they might hide in the grass along the riverbank. These animals have a powerful tail that helps them swim quickly through the water. Although they may look scary, alligators play an important role in nature. They help keep the number of fish and other animals in balance. Alligators have been around for millions of years, and they are a symbol of strength in the wild.

Questions:

1. Where do alligators live? _____

2. What do alligators use their sharp teeth for? _____

3. How does an alligator's tail help them? _____

4. Why is an alligator's skin important? _____

5. What role do alligators play in nature? _____

Reading Passage Activity

Crocodiles: Masters of the Water

 Crocodiles are ancient reptiles. They are typically found in freshwater habitats such as rivers, lakes, and swamps, as well as some brackish waters near coastlines. Crocodiles can be found in regions such as Africa, Asia, Australia, and the Americas. They are known for their powerful jaws and sharp teeth, which they use to catch prey like fish, birds, and even larger animals like antelope or buffalo.

Crocodiles are remarkable hunters, with excellent eyesight and the ability to stay still for long periods to ambush their prey. They also have tough, scaly skin that acts like armour, protecting them from harm and blending into their environment. Crocodiles use their long, muscular tails to propel themselves quickly through the water and to strike their prey when needed. These reptiles play a key role in their ecosystems by helping to control the populations of other animals, ensuring balance in the environment.

Although crocodiles are often seen as dangerous, they are an important part of nature and deserve respect for the role they play in the world.

Questions:

1). Where can crocodiles be found?

_____

2). What do crocodiles use their powerful jaws and sharp teeth for?

_____

3). How does a crocodile's tough, scaly skin help them?

_____

4). What role do crocodiles play in their ecosystem?

_____

5). How do crocodiles use their tails in the water?

_____

New Words:

Write the new words from the passage. Break them into syllables

if necessary. Now call the word/s for your teacher.

_____   _____

_____   _____

_____   _____

_____

Reminder:
Never stop improving
yourself.

CONSONANT BLENDS

 Consonant blends are also known as consonant clusters. They are groups of two or three consonants in a word that are pronounced together. Each consonant maintains its own sound. Unlike digraphs, where two consonants combine to make a single sound (e.g., "sh" in "ship"), consonant blends allow each consonant to be heard separately.

Examples of consonant blends are:

spr	gr	rk
tr	br	rp
bl	str	tw
sl	dw	lp
dr	sw	sm
gl	pl	thr
fl	nd	
fr	mp	
spl	sk	
cr	sc	

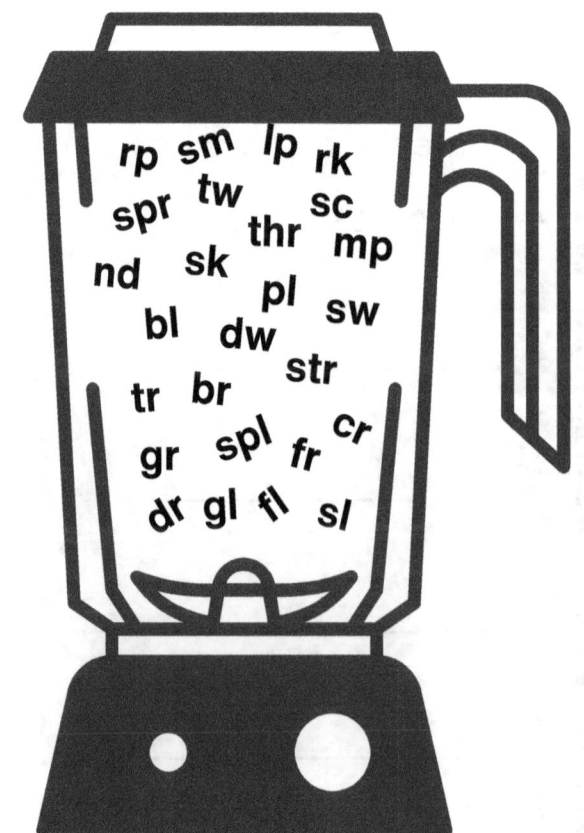

Types of Consonant Blends

There are three types of consonant blends. They are initial blends, final blends and three consonant blends.

1. **Initial Blends:** These occur at the beginning of words.
   - Examples:
     - "bl" as in "black"
     - "cr" as in "crab"
     - "st" as in "stop"
     - "tr" as in "tree"
2. **Final Blends:** These occur at the end of words.
   - Examples:
     - "nd" as in "sand"
     - "mp" as in "lamp"
     - "st" as in "last"
     - "lk" as in "milk"
3. **Three-Consonant Blends:** These involve three consonants that blend together while still allowing each sound to be heard.
   - Examples:
     - "str" as in "street"
     - "spl" as in "splash"
     - "spr" as in "spring"
     - "thr" as in "three"

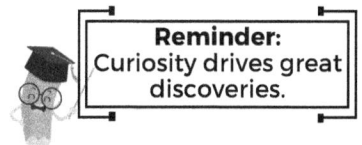

Reminder:
Curiosity drives great discoveries.

Initial Blends

Instruction: Write at least ten words for each initial consonant blend.

br	gr	pr	fr	dr
e.g. bread	e.g. grape	e.g. pray	e.g. frog	e.g. dream

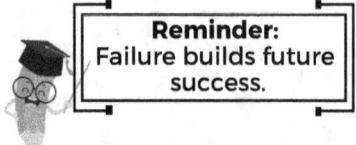

Reminder:
Failure builds future success.

bl	gl	pl	fl	sl
e.g. blood	e.g. glad	e.g. please	e.g. fling	e.g. sleep

sp	sw	sc	sm	sn
e.g. spoon	e.g. swell	e.g. scoop	e.g. smile	e.g. snail

Three Consonant Blends

Instruction: Write at least ten words for each three consonant blend.

scr	str	spr	spl	thr
e.g. screen	e.g. string	e.g. spring	e.g. splash	e.g. throat

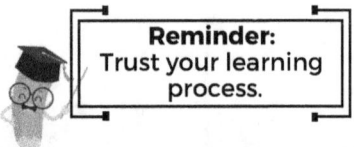

Reminder:
Trust your learning process.

Final Blend

Instruction: Write at least ten words for each final blend.

lk	nd	sk	mp	st
e.g. bulk	e.g. sand	e.g. flask	e.g. lamp	e.g. last

ft	rm	rp	lt	rt
e.g. left	e.g. harm	e.g. harp	e.g. halt	e.g. heart

Activity:

Instruction: Underline the **consonant blends** in each sentence. Write the words with the blends in your notebook. Know these words for spelling.

1. The strong wind blew the leaves across the street.

2. The cat jumped on the branch of the tree.

3. Frank found a crisp apple in his lunchbox.

4. The clock on the wall struck midnight.

5. Blake and his friend went to the splash park.

6. The frog leaped from the pond onto a plant.

7. The baker mixed the dough with a wooden spoon.

8. The skateboard slid down the steep ramp.

9. The child clapped his hands in excitement when he saw the

   flag wave.

10. Travis played his drum loudly in the school band.

SUFFIXES

A suffix is a syllable that is added at the end of a verb. It changes the verb from the present tense to the past.
The suffix -ed can make three sounds: /id/ /d/ and /t/.

The Three Sounds of the Suffix –ED

1. /id/

Rule: The "-ed" is pronounced as /ɪd/ or /ed/ when the verb ends in a "t" or "d" sound. This is because adding just a /t/ or /d/ would make the word difficult to pronounce, so a vowel sound is added.

Examples:
- "wanted" sounds like "wantid"
- "needed" sounds like "needid"
- "decided" sounds like "decidid"

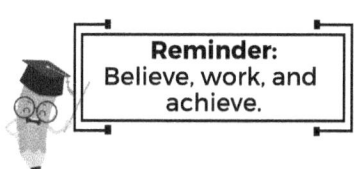
Reminder:
Believe, work, and achieve.

Activity:

Instruction: Make a list of at least 10 verbs each that end with T or D.

Verbs ending with t	Verbs ending with d

Activity:

Instruction: Identify the words in each column below.

ended	wanted
blended	hunted
needed	blotted
folded	parted
attended	waited
added	plotted
sounded	started
landed	visited
reminded	painted
guarded	greeted
tended	lifted
handed	shifted
bounded	accepted
lauded	stated

2. **/d/**

Rule: The "-ed" is pronounced as /d/ when the verb ends in a voiced consonant or a vowel sound. Voiced consonants involve the vibration of the vocal cords such as /l/v/m/r/b/n/g/w/y/z/.

Instruction: Write at least 6 verbs that end with each consonant.

L	V	R	M	B

N	W	G	Y	Z

Instructions:

Rewrite the words below then add the –ed to them. Call the words. If the verb ends with a consonant + y, drop the y, replace it with an "i" and add –ed. If the verb ends with a vowel + y, just add –ed.

L	V	R	M	B

N	W	G	Y	Z

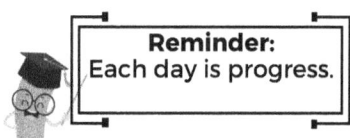

Reminder:
Each day is progress.

Instruction: Add –d or –ed to the following words that end in a vowel. Call the words for your teacher.

Teacher: Tick the box if the student called the word correctly. Put an X if it is incorrect.

1. echo _____ ☐

2. role _____ ☐

3. love _____ ☐

4. save _____ ☐

5. use _____ ☐

6. shave _____ ☐

7. atone _____ ☐

8. accuse _____ ☐

9. tiptoe _____ ☐

10. oppose _____ ☐

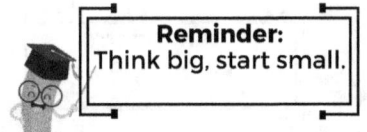

Reminder:
Think big, start small.

3. /t/

Rule: The "-ed" is pronounced as /t/ when the verb ends in a voiceless consonant, except for "t." Voiceless consonants do not use vocal cord vibration when pronounced: p, k, s, ch, sh, th, f, x, h.

Instruction: Call the words below.

skip	wish	puff
pick	kiss	box
flip	reach	bluff
kick	search	mix
grip	watch	brush
miss	push	relax
develop	snatch	tax
lock	sniff	fix
clip	finish	pack
pass	approach	finish
work	laugh	hack
stick	wash	relax
discuss	cough	alarm

Instruction: Rewrite each word then add –ed to them. In the case of those ending with p (except develop), double the ending consonant and then add –ed. Now call the new words.

skip _____	watch _____
pick _____	push _____
flip _____	snatch _____
kick _____	sniff _____
grip _____	finish _____
miss _____	approach _____
develop _____	laugh _____
lock _____	wash _____
clip _____	polish _____
pass _____	cough _____
work _____	puff _____
stick _____	box _____
guess _____	bluff _____
discuss _____	mix _____
wish _____	brush _____
kiss _____	relax _____
reach _____	tax _____
search _____	fix _____
pack _____	relax _____
finish _____	push _____
hack _____	alarm _____

Activity:

Instruction: Read each sentence then underline the verbs with the suffix –ed.

1). She laughed at the joke until her sides hurt.

2). They watched the sunset from the hill.

3). I finished my homework before going to bed.

4). He walked slowly to enjoy the cool breeze.

5). The children played outside all afternoon.

6). We painted the walls a bright blue.

7). She needed help with her science project.

8). They cooked a delicious dinner for the guests.

9). I talked to my friend about the upcoming trip.

10). He tried his best to complete the task.

11). The car stopped suddenly at the red light.

12). The teacher explained the lesson clearly.

13). She helped her brother with his homework.

14). We visited the museum last weekend.

15). He cleaned his room before leaving for school.

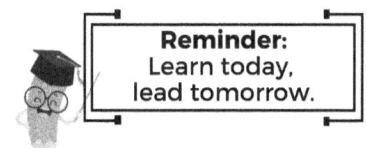

Reminder:
Learn today,
lead tomorrow.

SUFFIXES CONT'D

Suffixes are letters or groups of letters added to the end of a word to change its meaning.

Suffixes –tion and -sion

The suffixes **-sion**, and **-tion** are commonly used to form nouns from verbs. They typically indicate an action, state, or result of something. It is pronounced as **"shon/shun".**

1. **-tion**
   - How it is used: This is the most common suffix and is used when the root verb ends in -ate or when the root doesn't change.
   - What it means: It usually shows the act or result of something.

   Examples:
   - educate → education
   - create → creation

2. **-tion**
   - How it is used: This suffix is usually used when the root word ends in -de, -se, or -d.

- What it means: Similar to -tion, it shows the state, action, or result of something.

Examples:
- decide → decision
- revise → revision

Instruction: Change these verbs to nouns by dropping a letter or two and adding **–sion** or **–tion**. Your teacher will help you through the process.

educate → [   ]   convert → [   ]

create → [   ]   expand → [   ]

invent → [   ]   collide → [   ]

instruct → [   ]   persuade → [   ]

decorate → [   ]   divide → [   ]

organize → [   ]   confuse → [   ]

protect → [   ]   intrude → [   ]

decide → [   ]

The Suffix –ly

Words ending in **-ly** often describe how something is done.
Most words ending with **–ly** are called adverbs.
The **"ly"** at the end of adverbs are usually pronounced as "lee."
Call the words then discuss their meaning with your teacher.

suddenly	willingly	dangerously
sadly	carefully	happily
angrily	wonderfully	kindly
thankfully	badly	painfully
confidently	boldly	terribly
	peacefully	

Instruction: Write the root word for each adverb.

suddenly

_____

peacefully

_____

painfully

_____

happily

_____

angrily

_____

willingly

_____

wonderfully

_____

badly

_____

confidently

_____

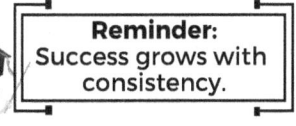

Reminder:
Success grows with
consistency.

Instruction: Read each sentence then underline the adverb. Discuss with the teacher the possible meaning of each word.

1). She spoke softly so she wouldn't wake the baby.

2). The cat moved silently across the room.

3). He answered the question quickly.

4). The children played happily in the park.

5). The teacher explained the lesson clearly.

6). The dog wagged its tail excitedly.

7). She worked carefully on her art project.

8). The wind blew gently through the trees.

9). He smiled warmly at his friends.

10). The clock ticked loudly in the quiet room.

11). She wrote the note neatly on the paper.

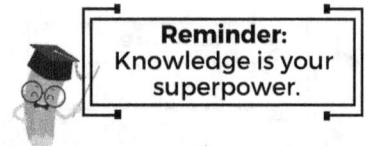

Reminder:
Knowledge is your
superpower.

The Suffix – ing

-ing is used to show a continuous action. It is also used like an adjective to describe something or a person.

Words with **–ing** are usually used with helping verbs

Examples: runn**ing**—This shows that an action is taking place and has not yet ended.
Amanda **is** *running* in the 100-metre race.
bor**ing**—This describes what someone thinks about something.
The game **is** very bor**ing**.

Instruction: Here is a list of some –ing words. Try to call them and then find the root word for each.

working	_____	singing	_____
running	_____	laughing	_____
reading	_____	jumping	_____
swimming	_____	shopping	_____
dancing	_____	cleaning	_____
cooking	_____	traveling	_____
writing	_____	hiking	_____
drawing	_____	playing	_____
studying	_____	biking	_____

Instruction: Create a tune for this very catchy jingle.

(Verse 1)

We're running, jumping, and playing all day,

Singing and dancing, we're making our way.

Cooking and eating, laughing with friends,

Life's full of fun that never quite ends!

(Chorus)

Swimming, shopping, and traveling too,

Drawing and writing, there's so much to do.

Gardening, cleaning, and hiking so high,

With all these activities, we're reaching the sky!

(Verse 2)

Reading and studying while watching the show,

Painting and biking, just let your joy flow.

From laughing to playing, every day's a delight,

With dancing and dreaming, everything feels right!

(Chorus)

Swimming, shopping, and traveling too,

Drawing and writing, there's so much to do.

Gardening, cleaning, and hiking so high,

With all these activities, we're reaching the sky!

The Suffix –ure

Rule: The suffix **"-ture"** or **"ure"** is used to form nouns that often mean **"the result of"** or **"how something is done** (the process) or **how something turns out to be** (the result, how it is or the state of it)". When **–ture/–ure** is added to a word, it often becomes a noun.

Examples: furni**ture**, plea**sure**, fail**ure**

Pronunciation: -ture is pronounced as "cher" as in chair.

Pronunciation: -ure can be pronounced as "yer/yur/your" as in "failure"

Pronunciation of words that have "s" affixed to –ure is "shaw" or "zher" as in "pleasure"

Instruction: Identify the words in the table. Add at least six more words to the list in your notebooks.

-ure	-sure	-ture
failure	pleasure	furniture
injure	measure	mixture
brochure	composure	agriculture

Instruction: Word Recognition—Colour the words as the teacher calls them. (Words with the -sure, -ure and -ture ending).

measure	failure	structure
pleasure	adventure	picture
closure	sculpture	future
exposure	nature	adventure
pressure	cure	furniture
treasure	lecture	culture
leisure	signature	creature
assure	manufacture	gesture
ensure	feature	mixture
enclosure	capture	agriculture

Instruction: Read the sentences aloud then put a circle around the words with the –ture, -sure or –ure affixes.

1). We need to measure the table before buying a new one.

2). The doctor will ensure you are feeling better.

3). Marion found great pleasure in reading her favourite book.

4). The pressure in the tire was too low.

5). The pirate hid the treasure on the island.

6). The failure of the test made him study harder.

7). The old bridge has a strong structure.

8). She took a picture of the sunset.

9). The creature crawled slowly across the grass.

10). The future of the planet depends on us.

11). The classroom has very comfortable furniture.

12). The medicine will help to cure the cold.

13). Jim looked forward to a life full of adventure.

14). The artist created a beautiful sculpture from clay.

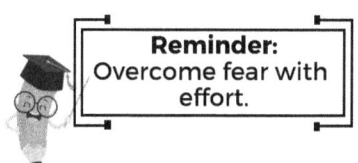

Reminder:
Overcome fear with effort.

Instruction: Use context clues in the sentences on page 145 to say what the words on the left mean. Write your answer in the column on the right.

adventure	
failure	
cure	
pleasure	
sculpture	
structure	

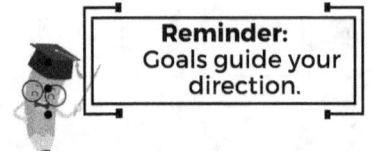

Reminder:
Goals guide your
direction.

The Suffixes –s and –es

Both **-s** and **-es** are used to form the plurals of nouns and the singular verbs.

-s can have three different pronunciations depending on the ending sound of the word:

- **"-s" is pronounced /s/**: After voiceless consonants which include /f/k/p/s/t/th/.

   (e.g., cats, bosses, cloths, ticks)

- **"-s" is pronounced /z/** after voiced consonants and vowels: These consonants cause your voice box to vibrate. They include: /b/, /d/, /g/, /m/, /n/, /l/, /r/, /v/, /z/, /w/ng/th/ and /ʒ/ (as in 'vision')

   (e.g., dogs pronounced dogz; rams pronounced ramz)

- **" -es" pronounced /ɪz/** after words ending in s, sh, ch, x, or z.

   (e.g., washes /ˈwɒshɪz/, churches /churchiz)

"s" pronounced /s/	"s" pronounced /z/	"es" pronounced /iz/
cats	dogs	brushes
books	books	boxes
hats	rivers	matches
beds	toys	classes
parks	cars	buses
cups	waves	buzzes
toys	games	kisses
rocks	friends	dishes
nights	boys	taxes
pencils	leaves	passes
paths	lambs	horses

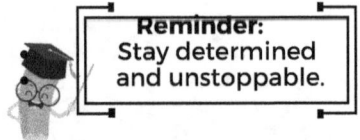

Reminder:
Stay determined
and unstoppable.

Instruction: Write a sentence using each of the following words. Be sure to use the word correctly and include the -s or -es suffix.

1). **foxes:**

_____

_____

_____

2). **houses:**

_____

_____

_____

3). **dishes:**

_____

_____

_____

4). **stars:**

_____

_____

_____

5). **pencils:**

_____

_____

_____

Activity:

Instruction: Read each sentence carefully. Be sure to pronounce the words in bold correctly.

Teacher: Tick the box if the words in bold are pronounced correctly.

1). The **cats** chased each other around the yard. ☐

2). We need to pack the **boxes** before we move. ☐

3). The **dogs** barked loudly at the mail carrier. ☐

4). The **buses** were delayed because of the rain. ☐

5). She made three **wishes** on her birthday cake. ☐

6). My **friends** and I played a game of soccer. ☐

7). The artist cleaned her **brushes** after painting. ☐

8). The **trees** in the park were covered in snow. ☐

9). He read five **books** during summer vacation. ☐

10). They gave each other sweet **kisses** before bedtime. ☐

11). The **foxes** came out to play at dusk. ☐

12). They painted the new **houses** on their street. ☐

13). After the meal, she dried the **dishes**. ☐

14). The **stars** twinkled in the night sky. ☐

15). We sharpened our **pencils** for the test. ☐

Prefixes im-, in-, il-, dis-, un-, ir-

A prefix is a syllable that is placed at the beginning of a word. It changes the meaning of the word.

The prefixes **im-, il-, ir-, un-, dis-,** and **in-** are all used to form words that indicate the opposite or absence of something which often means "not" or "the reverse of.

- **-im** means "not" or "opposite of" and is used with words beginning with **m** and **p.**

- **-in** means "not" or "opposite of" and is used with some **adjectives** and **nouns.**

- **-dis** means "Not," "opposite of," or "reverse of" and used with a wide variety of **adjectives, adverbs**, and some **nouns.**

- **-il** means "not" or "opposite of" and is used with words beginning with **l.**

- **-ir** means "not" or "opposite of" and is used with words beginning with **r.**

- **-un** means "not" or "opposite of" and is used with a variety of **adjectives, adverb** and **verbs.**

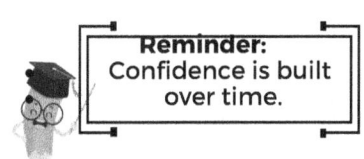

Reminder:
Confidence is built
over time.

Instruction: Call the following words.

legal	perfect
literate	mobile
logical	patient
luminate	mortal
regular	happy
responsible	fair
relevant	certain
repairable	usual
possible	tidy
agree	honest
connect	like
appear	accurate
capable	secure
active	considerate

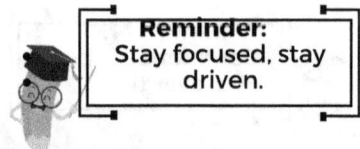

Reminder:
Stay focused, stay driven.

Instruction: Write the meanings of the words on the left in the right column.

Word	Meaning
legal	
literate	
logical	
mortal	
mobile	
happy	
honest	
repairable	
possible	
agree	
accurate	

Instruction: Write the opposite of each word using **im-, ir-, il-, un-, dis- or in-.** What is the new word? Call them for the teacher.

Word	Opposite
perfect	
mobile	
patient	
mortal	
happy	
fair	
certain	
usual	
tidy	
honest	
accurate	

Word	Opposite
legal	
literate	
logical	
luminate	
regular	
responsible	
relevant	
repairable	
possible	
agree	
connect	
appear	
capable	

Activity:

Instruction: Write what the following words mean on the line.

1). illegal: _____

2). unhappy: _____

3). disagree: _____

4). irresponsible: _____

5). incapable: _____

6). disunity: _____

7). disappear: _____

8). imperfect: _____

9). immobile: _____

10). unprepared: _____

Instruction: Use 5 of the new words that you have made to create simple sentences.

1).

_____

_____

2).

_____

_____

3).

_____

_____

4).

_____

_____

5).

_____

_____

Prefixes re and pre

re-

The prefix **re-** means "again" or "back." It shows that something is being done a second time or that it is returning to a previous state or condition.

Examples:

return	repair	replay
receive	revisit	redeem
recycle	rearrange	recycle
reread	rewrite	repaint
reclaim	redo	replace
recover	rebuild	recall

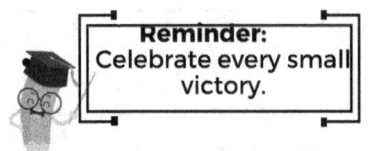

Reminder:
Celebrate every small victory.

Instruction: Match the word on the left with its correct meaning on the right by writing the correct letter.

Word	Meaning
rebuild _____	(A). to visit again
replay _____	(B). to use again
rewind _____	(C). to start again
rewrite _____	(D). to do again
revisit _____	(E). to play again
recycle _____	(F). to build again
restart _____	(G). to fill again
redo _____	(H). to wind back
refill _____	(I). to write again
recover _____	(J). to get back or regain

pre-

The prefix **pre-** means **"before"** or **"earlier."** It means that something happens before a specific time or event

Examples:

prepare	preschool	prepaid
predict	pretend	presume
prelude	preliminary	premature
preplan	prearrange	preapprove
precaution	preorder	pretest

Instruction: Write the correct word for each clue.

> prepare   prepaid   predict   premature   pre-plan
> pre-arrange   pre-heat   precaution   pre-order   pre-test

1. To heat before _____

2. To plan before _____

3. To pay before the time _____

4. To put something in place before the time _____

5. A test given before the main test? _____

6. To order before time? _____

7. To say what will happen before it happens _____

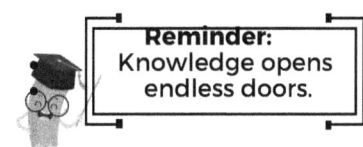

SYLLABICATION RULES

Syllabication is the process of dividing words into syllables, which are the basic units of sound in speech. Understanding the rules of syllabication helps with reading, pronunciation, and spelling.

> **syl/la/ble**

Look at the word in the rectangle. What has happened to it?

Yes, it has been separated into parts. The parts are called syllables. A syllable is a part of a word with a single vowel sound.

A syllable must always have a vowel. A vowel can function as a syllable but consonants by themselves cannot.

Example: ba/na/na
A syllable is considered as a beat. There can be one or more than one beats in a word. For example, in the word "apple," there are two syllables or beats: "ap-ple." You can clap along with each syllable to hear the beats: clap for "ap" and clap for "ple."

Similarly, the word "banana" has three syllables or beats: "ba-na-na," where you can clap three times, one for each syllable.

When you call a word, your mouth opens and your jaw drops. Every time that your jaw drops, you produce a syllable or a beat.

- **Rule 1:** Every syllable has one vowel sound.
  A syllable contains one vowel sound, which may be a single vowel (e.g., "cat") or a vowel combination (e.g., "rain").

  Example:
  - cat (1 syllable)
  - a-bout (2 syllables)
  - ex-am-ple (3 syllables)

- **Rule 2:** Split between two consonants.
  When two consonants come between two vowels, divide the word between the consonants.

  Example:
  - nap-kin
  - sis-ter
  - bas-ket

  Exception: Do not divide consonant blends or digraphs (like th, ch, sh, wh, ph, bl, cl).
  - bush-el
  - ath-lete

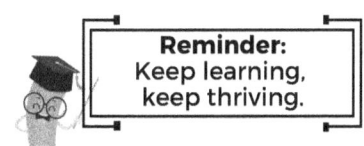

Reminder:
Keep learning,
keep thriving.

Rule 3: Divide between a prefix and a root word.
Always divide a word between a prefix and the root word.

Example:
- un-tie
- pre-test
- re-play

Rule 4: Divide between a root word and a suffix.
Divide between the root word and suffix, especially if the suffix begins with a consonant.

Example:
- hope-ful
- quick-ly
- care-less

Exception: Do not divide before a suffix that begins with a vowel, such as -ing or -ed.
- read-ing
- talk-ing
- play-ed

Rule 5: Split between two vowels that do not form a diphthong or vowel team.
When two vowels next to each other do not make one sound (i.e., they are not a diphthong or vowel team), divide between the vowels.

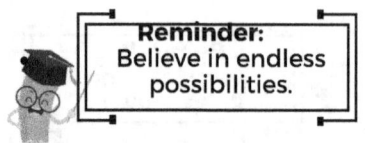

Reminder:
Believe in endless possibilities.

Example:

- di-et
- li-ar
- po-et

Rule 6: Keep diphthongs and vowel teams together.
Do not split a syllable where vowels work together to form one sound, as in diphthongs or vowel teams.

Example:

- boat
- rain
- loud

Rule 7: Split compound words between the two words.

Example:

- sun-set
- tooth-brush
- foot-ball

Rule 8: Silent "e" stays with the previous syllable.
In words with a silent e, the e remains part of the syllable with the previous consonant and vowel.

Example:

- date
- bake
- hope-ful

- **Rule 9:** Consonant-le syllables.
  In words that end with a consonant + le, divide the word before the consonant-le.

  Example:
  - ta-ble
  - lit-tle
  - gig-gle

- **Rule 10:** One consonant between two vowels usually joins the second vowel.
  When a single consonant comes between two vowels, it usually goes with the second vowel, unless the first vowel is short.

  Example:
  - ti-ger
  - ba-by
  - o-pen

- **Rule 11:** Vowel-consonant-consonant-vowel (VCCV) Rule
  When the pattern is vowel-consonant-consonant-vowel, divide between the consonants.

  Example:
  - pic-nic
  - hap-py
  - mon-key

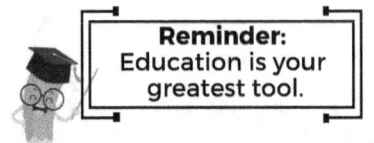

Reminder:
Education is your
greatest tool.

Rule 12: Closed Syllable Rule

A syllable is closed when it ends in a consonant, making the vowel sound short.

Example:
- cat
- sun
- top

Rule 13: Open Syllable Rule

A syllable is open when it ends in a vowel, which makes the vowel sound long.

Example:
- ba-by
- ti-ger
- pa-per

Rule 14: Syllable Stress

Words with two syllables often place stress on the first syllable, especially in nouns and adjectives.

Example:
- ta-ble
- win-dow
- hap-py

In verbs and some other words, the second syllable is often stressed.
- be-gin
- a-bout
- de-cide

Exercises for Syllabication

Rule 1: Every syllable must have a vowel/one vowel sound.

Instruction: Look at each word below. Break the word into its syllables by placing a hyphen between them. For example, "elephant" becomes "el-e-phant."

Write the words in the correct column based on how many syllables they have.

butterfly   dog   apple   elephant   pencil
giraffe   computer   tree   watermelon   rocket

1 Syllable	2 Syllables	3 Syllables	4 Syllables	5 Syllables

Instruction: Below is a list of words. Split each word into its syllables by placing a slash (/) between them. For example, "chocolate" becomes "cho/co/late."

After splitting the words, write the number of syllables.

Word	Split the Word	Number of Syllables
fantastic	_____	_____
rainbow	_____	_____
octopus	_____	_____
basketball	_____	_____
kitten	_____	_____
refrigerator	_____	_____
triangle	_____	_____
lamp	_____	_____
astronaut	_____	_____
television	_____	_____

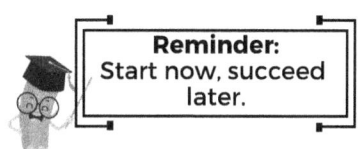

Reminder:
Start now, succeed later.

Rule 2: When two consonants come between two vowels, divide the word between the consonants. Do not divide consonant blends or digraphs (like th, ch, sh, wh, ph, bl, cl).

Instruction: Divide the words by applying the above rule.

Word	Syllabication
batter	_____
better	_____
happy	_____
picnic	_____
ginger	_____
summer	_____
kitten	_____
rampant	_____
commune	_____
party	_____
carry	_____
under	_____
monkey	_____
sister	_____

Rule 3: Divide between prefix and a root word.

Instruction:

- Draw a vertical line between the prefix and the root word on the line provided.
- Write the meaning of the word based on the prefix and root word.

1. redo: _____ ☐

2. unkind: _____ ☐

3. dislike: _____ ☐

4. preheat: _____ ☐

5. revisit: _____ ☐

6. inaccurate: _____ ☐

7. impossible: _____ ☐

8. prepay: _____ ☐

9. disagree: _____ ☐

10. unpack: _____ ☐

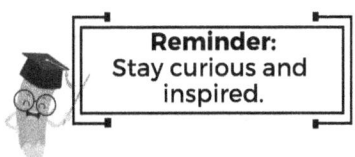

Reminder:
Stay curious and inspired.

Rule 4: Divide between a root word and a suffix.

Instruction:
- Draw a vertical line (/) between the root word and the suffix.
- Write the meaning of the word by combining the root word and the suffix.

1. helpful   _____   [ ]

2. caring   _____   [ ]

3. quickly   _____   [ ]

4. endless   _____   [ ]

5. darkness   _____   [ ]

6. taller   _____   [ ]

7. joyful   _____   [ ]

8. thankful   _____   [ ]

9. kindness   _____   [ ]

10. teacher   _____   [ ]

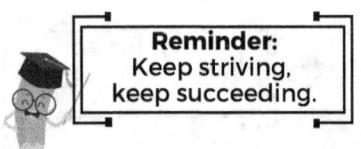

Reminder:
Keep striving,
keep succeeding.

Rule 5: Split between two vowels that do not form a diphthong or vowel team.

Instructions:

- Separate the word between the two vowels that do not form a diphthong or vowel team.
- Write the two syllables separately.
- Read each word aloud after dividing it.

Word	Two Syllables
diet	_____
quiet	_____
cruel	_____
ruin	_____
poem	_____
idea	_____
fluent	_____
radio	_____
duo	_____
react	_____

Rule 6: Do not split a syllable where vowels work together to form one sound, as in diphthongs or vowel teams.

Instruction:

Separate the following words into syllables.

1. towel   _____

2. esteem   _____

3. sweetest   _____

4. reason   _____

5. sailor   _____

6. relief   _____

7. rooster   _____

8. training   _____

9. coat   _____

10. receive   _____

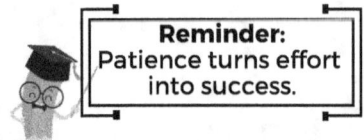

Reminder:
Patience turns effort into success.

Instructions:

- Find five more words with diphthongs or vowel teams.
- Write the words then divide them into syllables.
- Explain to your teacher how you kept the diphthongs or vowel teams together.

Word	Syllabication

Rule 7: Split compound words between the two words. Remember that compound words are two different words put together to make one.

Instruction:

Write as many compound words in the boxes below then break them into syllables.

tooth/brush		

Rule 8: Silent e stays with the previous syllable. Divide the word so that the silent e remains part of the syllable with the previous consonant and vowel.

Instructions:

Divide these words correctly by applying the rule above.

toenail   hopeful   lonely   alone   provoke
cone   divide   tadpole   homeward   dribble

Rule 9: In words that end with a consonant + le, divide the word before the consonant-le.

Instruction:
- Identify the words below. Divide the words into syllables, ensuring the -le forms its own syllable with the previous consonant.
- Write the syllables on the line provided.

1. bubble   _____

2. fable   _____

3. giggle   _____

4. title   _____

5. maple   _____

6. simple   _____

7. puzzle   _____

8. jungle   _____

9. cradle   _____

10. handle   _____

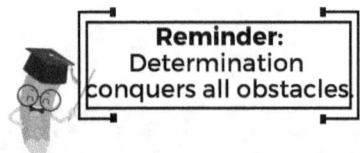

Reminder:
Determination
conquers all obstacles

Rule 10: When a single consonant comes between two vowels, it usually goes with the second vowel, unless the first vowel is short.

Instructions:

Identify these words then divide them into syllables using the rule above.

> tiger   blazer   cosy   later   miser   silent   donut
> behave   nature   spider   rumour   moment   tutor
> before   navy   nasal   wiper   halo   broken   notice

_____   _____

_____   _____

_____   _____

_____   _____

_____   _____

_____   _____

_____   _____

_____   _____

Rule 11: When the pattern is vowel-consonant-consonant-vowel (VCCV), divide between the two consonants.

Instruction:

Divide the following words into syllables. Use the rule above as a guide.

puppet	
ladder	
winter	
hammer	
cotton	
tennis	
letter	
hidden	
basket	
butter	

STRATEGIES FOR ATTACKING NEW WORDS

📌 Never allow a new word to attack you. Attack the words using the following strategies:

Look for the vowels or if they are paired. If they are paired you are going to get a different sound. The sounds could be long for example "boat" or you might get two different sounds as in "coin"

Look for the whole word.

Look for letters that you can identify and sound them

Look how many vowels are in the word. It will tell you how many syllables are in the word or if the vowels are long or short in/com/plete

Break the words into syllables if this is possible and cover each part with your finger as you call each part. Blend them together ba/by=baby

If it is a one syllable word, point to each letter, sound them out. (Remember, digraphs/diphthongs stay together. Now blend them together. b-r-oo-m=broom

KEY TO PRONUNCIATIONS OF CONSONANTS

Bb

b says **/b/** as in ball, book
bb says **/b/** as in hobby
bt says /t/ in doubt
mb says /m/ in thumb

Cc

c says **/k/** as in cat
c says **/sh/** as in appreciate
c softens to **/s/** when followed by E, I or Y as in cent, science, cycle

Dd

d says **/d/** as in dog
dd says **/d/** as in daddy

Ff

f says **/f/** as in fan
f ff says **/f/** as in jiffy
f says **/f/** as in half
ph says **/f/** as in phone
-gh says **/f/** as in cough

Gg

g says **/g/** as in gas
gg says **/g/** as in giggle
gh- says **/g/** as in ghost
gu- says **/g/** as in guide
g says **/zh/** in regime (rare)
G is softened to **/j/** when followed by **E, I** or **Y** as in gem, gym, gin

Hh

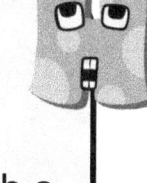

h says **/h/** as in hole
h is often combined with a few consonant sounds as a silent letter - as in g**h**ost - or representing a digraph sound - as in **ph**one or rou**gh**

Jj

j says **/j/** as in jet

-g -ge & **-dge** can also give you the **/j/** sound as in gem, siege, edge

Kk

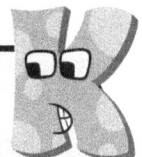

k says **/k/** as in kick
-ck says **/k/** as in sack
k is silent when it is **followed by n** as in k**n**ow, and k**n**ot
c ch & **-que** can also make the **/k/** sound

Ll

l says **/l/** as in log
ll says **/l/** as in lollipop
-le says **/l/** as in simple
lf says **/f/** in calf and half
al says **/aw/** in walk
oul makes the short /oo/ in would

Mm

m is **/m/** in **m**ilk
mm is **/m/** in su**mm**er
mb is **/m/** in thu**mb**
-mn is **/m/** in autu**mn**
m is always /m/, **except** when it comes at the beginning of a word and is followed by **n** like in the word **mnemonic**

Nn

n says /n/ as in nail
n says /n/ as in tank
nn is /n/ in bunny
kn says /n/ as in knee
gn says /n/ as in gnash
pn says /n/ in pneumonia

Pp

p says /p/ as in pie
pp says /p/ as in puppy
p is silent in pn- and ps-
words as in pneumonia and
psychosis

Qq

q- says /kw/ as in quick
but, -que says /k/ as in
cheque
q always goes along with u
and so u in this case it is not
considered a vowel.

Rr

r is /r/ as in run
rr is /r/ as in worry
rh is /r/ as in rhyme
wr is /r/ as in wring
When the vowels come
before the r as in ar, er, ir, or,
ur, the vowels are controlled
by the r and the r will
produce varied sounds. (See
r-controlled vowels)

Ss

s says /s/ in sing
except in the following
cases:
s says /sh/ as in sure
s says /zh/ as in casual
s says /z/ as in is
ss says /sh/ as in pressure
-se says /z/ as in choose

Tt

t says /t/ in tall
t says /ch/ in nature
t says /sh/ in initiate
-bt says /t/ in doubt
tt says /t/ in litter
ti- says /sh/ in station

Vv

v says **/v/** as in **v**ideo
-ve says **/v/** as in beha**ve**
f says **/v/** as in o**f**
(this is irregular)

Ww

w is **/w/** as in **w**atch
wh are **/w/** as in **wh**at
wh is **/hw/** as in **wh**ile
wh is **/h/** as in **wh**ole
wr is **/r/** as in **wr**ist

Xx

x says **/ks/** as in ja**x**
x says **/gz/** if it comes before
a stressed syllable as in
e**x**ample
x says **/z/** if it begins a word
as in **x**erox and is in the
middle of a word such as
lu**x**ury
x says /k/ sound followed by
/sh/ in words such as
comple**x**ion
x says /e/ followed by **/ks/**
such as **x**-ray

Yy

y says "**ye**" at the start of a
word such as **y**et & **y**ellow
y says **/ī/** in at the end of a
one syllable word such as cr**y**
or sh**y**.
y says "**e**" in two syllable
words such a happ**y**

Zz

z is **/z/** in **z**oo
zz is **/z/** in fu**zz**y
-ze is **/z/** in snoo**ze**
z is **/zh/** in sei**z**ure

SIGHT WORD VOCABULARY

Pre-primer

a	and	away	big	can	come	for
funny	go	if	here	I	in	it
jump	little	look	make	me	my	not
one	play	red	run	said	see	the
three	to	two	up	we	where	you
was	am	girl	do	no		

Primer

all	are	am	ate	be	but	came
did	do	eat	get	he	have	like
into	must	now	new	our	pretty	saw
say	she	so	soon	there	they	that

Primer Cont'd

them	under	want	was	too	with	what
went	who	will	good	yes	well	please

Grade 1

of	his	had	him	her	some	as
when	could	were	them	ask	an	over
just	from	any	how	know	put	take
every	old	by	after	think	let	going
walk	again	may	stop	fly	round	give
once	open	has	live	thank	went	come

Grade 2

would	very	your	its	around	down	right
green	their	call	sleep	five	wash	or
before	been	off	cold	tell	work	does
goes	first	write	always	made	gave	us

Grade 2 Cont'd

buy	those	use	fast	pull	both	sit
which	read	why	found	because	best	upon
these	wish	many	sing			

Grade 3

could	long	about	got	six	together	myself
start	clean	carry	better	bring	about	laugh
only	pick	try	today	done	hurt	light
full	cut	small	own	show	far	hot
draw	shall	eight	drink	seven	grow	warm
wash	draw	across	mother	important	listen	family
me	found					

Grade 4

frighten	house	explain	enough	without	children	sometimes
favourite	leave	beacuse	being	beautiful	though	different
between	school	people	watch	through	answer	those
family	should	chimney	outside	suppose	grew	something
whisper	wonder	early	without	grew	broken	breakfast
himself	cover	country	dream	matter	world	nothing
few	field	should				

Sight Word List- Grade 5

accident	fork	rug	bandage
class	month	tear	crayons
follow	root	answer	grade
mind	talk	cough	none
road	against	gate	sandwich
sugar	company	napkin	thousand
ache	forth	ruler	bank
clear	mountain	thanksgiving	crowd
forget	rose	arm	grain
minute	taste	cousin	noon
room	alone	glad	scissors
summer	copy	neither	throat
act	furniture	sail	bathe
cloth	move	thick	crown
forgot	rubber	automobile	great
mirror	teacher	crackers	nor
rooster	already	golden	scooter
sweater	cost	nickel	thumb
afternoon	garage	salt	beautiful
cocoa	music	thirsty	cry
grocery	serve	dining	shoulder
	tomorrow	ice	twenty

Sight Word List- Grade 5

north	blackboard	ought	broom
season	date	ship	double
tire	heard	towel	juice
begin	office	body	pants
cupboard	several	dinner	sick
guess	tongue	indoors	ugly
note	bleed	outdoors	bump
self	dentist	shirt	drawer
toe	heart	train	knee
begun	often	bow	pass
curtain	shadow	dirt	silk
hammer	touch	instead	umbrella
nurse	blind	overalls	burnt
sent	die	short	drug
tomatoes	hour	tub	lady
believe	other	bridge	past
danger	shape	doctor	sir
handkerchief	tough	iron	until
ocean	blood	pain	butcher
size	valley	paste	each

EASY-TO- FOLLOW RULES
FOR PHONEME SEGMENTATION

Listen for Sounds, Not Letters

We are not worried about spelling here, just what we hear. Even if a word has five letters, it might only have three sounds! "fish" has 3 sounds: /f/ /i/ /sh/ (not 4-even though it has 4 letters.)

Double Letters = One Sound

When you see double letters like ll or ss, just remember: They make one sound, not two.

spell
/s/p/e/l/

Watch Out for Diagraphs (Two Letters = One Sound)

Some letter pairs—like sh, ch, th, ph—make just one sound. We call these digraphs. "ship" = /sh/ /i/ /p/ (3 sounds, not 4)

ship
/sh/i/p/

Blends = Separate Sounds

If two consonants are side by side and you can hear both sounds, it is a blend. "stop"= /s/ /t/ /o/ /p/. You can hear both /s/ and /t/ clearly.

/s/t/o/p/

EASY-TO- FOLLOW RULES
FOR PHONEME SEGMENTATION

eat
/ē/t/

Easy Vowel Sound Count

Whether the vowel is long or short, if it makes a sound, it counts as a phoneme. "eat" = /e/ /t/ (2 sounds)

simple
/s/i/m/p/l

Consonant + le = A Chunk that Sounds Like "ul"

Words that end with consonant + le (like simple, little, or bubble) usually end with the sound /əl/ - it's like saying "ul".

knee
/n/ē/

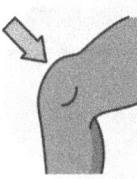

Silent Letters Don't Count

If you can't hear it, you don't count it. Simple as that. "Knee" = /n/ /e/ (only 2 sounds- "k" is silent)

SUPPLEMENTARY ACTIVITIES

By providing a range of supplementary activities alongside core literacy tasks, teachers can create a robust, supportive learning environment that scaffolds and reinforces literacy concepts, ensuring long-term retention and deeper understanding for all students.

Here are a few ways in which that could be done:

Differentiated Learning:

Students learn at varying paces and in different ways, so supplementary activities provide opportunities to tailor instruction to individual needs. By offering additional reading games, writing exercises, or group work, teachers can reinforce difficult concepts and allow students to practice skills in diverse ways.

Reinforcement Through Multi-Sensory Learning:

Supplementary activities like hands-on tasks, visual aids, and interactive tools (such as flashcards, manipulatives, or digital resources) engage multiple senses, which can help reinforce and retain literacy concepts more effectively than standard worksheets or lessons alone.

Extended Practice:

Literacy activities often introduce foundational skills, but students need extended practice to master them. Supplementary activities such as reading aloud, partner discussions, or word-building games provide additional exposure, helping students move from basic understanding to fluency.

Application in Real-Life Contexts:

Supplementary activities that mimic real-world situations (like writing letters, reading recipes, or conducting interviews) allow students to apply literacy concepts in meaningful contexts, thereby deepening their understanding and making the learning more relevant and memorable.

Engagement and Motivation:

By incorporating creative and interactive supplementary activities such as storytelling sessions, literacy-based scavenger hunts, or group projects, teachers can boost student engagement. Higher engagement increases motivation, helping students commit to practicing literacy skills.

Formative Assessment Opportunities:

Supplementary activities give teachers an informal way to assess students' grasp of literacy concepts. Activities like peer teaching, quizzes, or small group discussions allow teachers to observe areas where students may need more support and adjust instruction accordingly.

Varied Approaches to Mastery:

Some students may need more time or different approaches to grasp certain literacy concepts. Supplementary activities such as role-play, songs, or journaling provide alternative approaches, ensuring that every student has a chance to achieve mastery through methods that resonate with them.

Building Independence and Confidence:

As students engage in supplementary literacy activities, they gradually build confidence in their abilities. Independent reading tasks, spelling challenges, or creative writing prompts encourage students to apply their knowledge without constant guidance, fostering self-directed learning and reinforcing concepts at their own pace.

Helpful Websites

Here are some highly useful websites that provide activities and resources for literacy development. These websites can greatly support literacy instruction by providing fun, interactive, and educational activities that engage students in various aspects of reading, writing, and language learning.

- **Bookfusion**
  Website: https://www.bookfusion.com/libraries
  Description: BookFusion is a digital reading platform that provides a seamless reading experience across multiple devices. It allows users to read, organize, and share eBooks in various formats, while also offering features like annotations, bookmarks, and offline access. BookFusion caters to individual readers, schools, and businesses, with options to create reading groups, share content, and track reading progress.

- **Wordwall**
  Website: https://wordwall.net/en-us/community/games
  Description: Wordwall is an online tool that helps teachers create interactive activities like quizzes and word searches. It offers customizable templates and pre-made resources for various subjects and can be used both online and offline. Wordwall enhances classroom learning by making lessons more engaging and interactive.

- **ReadWriteThink**
  Website: https://www.readwritethink.org/
  Description: ReadWriteThink offers free lesson plans, student interactives, and printable worksheets for teachers, focusing on reading and writing activities. There are resources for all grade levels with interactive tools to help reinforce literacy concepts.

- **Starfall**

  Website: https://www.starfall.com

  Description: Starfall is an interactive platform designed to help young learners with reading, phonics, and basic literacy skills through engaging, interactive games and activities. It's particularly helpful for Pre-K to Grade 2 students.

- **ABCya!**

  Website: https://www.abcya.com/

  Description: ABCya! provides interactive games that focus on literacy, spelling, grammar, and vocabulary. It's ideal for students from Kindergarten to Grade 5 and makes learning fun through gameplay.

- **Storyline Online**

  Website: https://storylineonline.net/

  Description: Storyline Online features videos of popular children's books being read aloud by celebrities. This is a great tool for reading comprehension, listening skills, and vocabulary development for elementary students.

- **Oxford Owl**

  Website: https://www.oxfordowl.co.uk/

  Description: Oxford Owl provides free ebooks, literacy games, and resources for parents and teachers. It also offers advice on how to teach literacy skills at home or in the classroom, perfect for children aged 3-11.

- **Education.com**

  Website: https://www.education.com/

  Description: This site offers a wide range of worksheets, lesson plans, games, and activities focusing on reading, writing, spelling, and grammar. It caters to various age groups from Kindergarten through Grade 5.

- **Epic!**
  Website: https://www.getepic.com/
  Description: Epic! is a digital library that provides unlimited access to thousands of high-quality books, audiobooks, and learning videos for kids 12 and under. Teachers can assign reading activities and track progress.

- **Teach Your Monster to Read**
  Website: https://www.teachyourmonster.org/
  Description: This game-based website helps children learn phonics and reading fundamentals. It's a great tool for early readers and uses fun characters and interactive gameplay to teach literacy concepts.

- **Scholastic**
  Website: https://export.scholastic.com/en
  Description: Scholastic offers a variety of literacy resources, including lesson plans, book lists, printables, and interactive activities. It's great for teachers looking to supplement classroom instruction with engaging literacy content.

- **Funbrain**
  Website: https://www.funbrain.com
  Description: Funbrain provides literacy-focused games, books, and videos for children in Pre-K through Grade 8. The activities are designed to make learning fun while reinforcing reading and writing skills.

- **Games to Learn English**
  Website: https://www.gamestolearnenglish.com/
  Description: This website offers free resources for students to learn English online. It includes a variety of games that make practicing English enjoyable and engaging.

References & Acknowledgement

Dobbs Santos, S. (2012). Phonological awareness interventions. Retrieved from https://www.ambridge.k12.pa.us/wp-content/uploads/2020/07/Phonological-Awareness-Interventions.pdf

Francisco, C. (n.d.). What is a diphthong? Literacy intervention tips and tricks. Retrieved October 8, 2024, from http://literacytipsandtricks.weebly.com/what-is-a-diphthong.html

Heggerty, M. (2015). Phonemic awareness screener assessment. Literacy Resources Inc.

Teacher Lindsey. (2020, October 22). What is phonics? Retrieved from https://teacher-lindsey.com/what-is-phonics/

WETA. (2024). Basics: Phonological and phonemic awareness. Reading Rockets: Launching Young Readers. Retrieved from https://www.reading rockets.org/reading-101/reading-and-writing-basics/phonological-and-phonemic-awareness

Winter, C. (2021, July 19). Word mapping activities: Connecting phonemes to graphemes. Lead in Literacy - Resources for Kindergarten, 1st & 2nd Grade. Retrieved from https://leadinliteracy.com/phoneme-grapheme-word-mapping-activities/

7-syllables-blog-pic.png (PNG Image, 776 × 1008 pixels) – Scaled (62%). (2013). Retrieved from https://blog.maketaketeach.com/wp-content/uploads/2013/12/7-syllables-blog-pic.png

Phonological awareness intervention screening. (n.d.). Retrieved October 8, 2024, from https://www.fullertonsd.org/cms/lib/CA50010905/Centricity/Domain/1993/PA_Intervention_Screening.pdf

Some portions of this book were developed with the help of AI-based suggestions generated by OpenAI's ChatGPT.

WORD BUILDING ACTIVITY WITH ONSET CARDS AND WORD FAMILIES (RIMES)

Cut out the onset cards and use them in combination with the word family/rime cards to create as many words as possible. You can form both real and nonsense words.

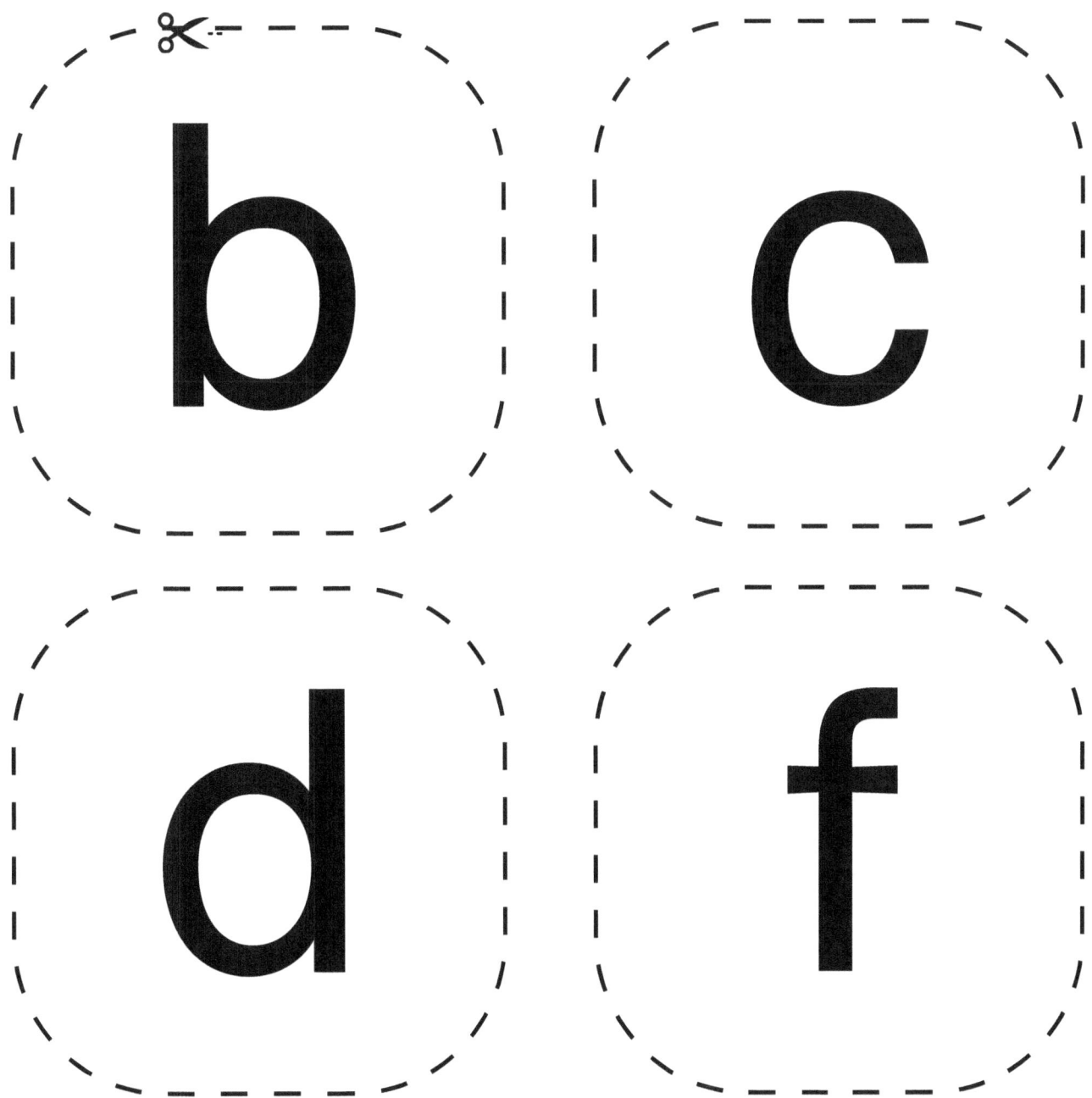

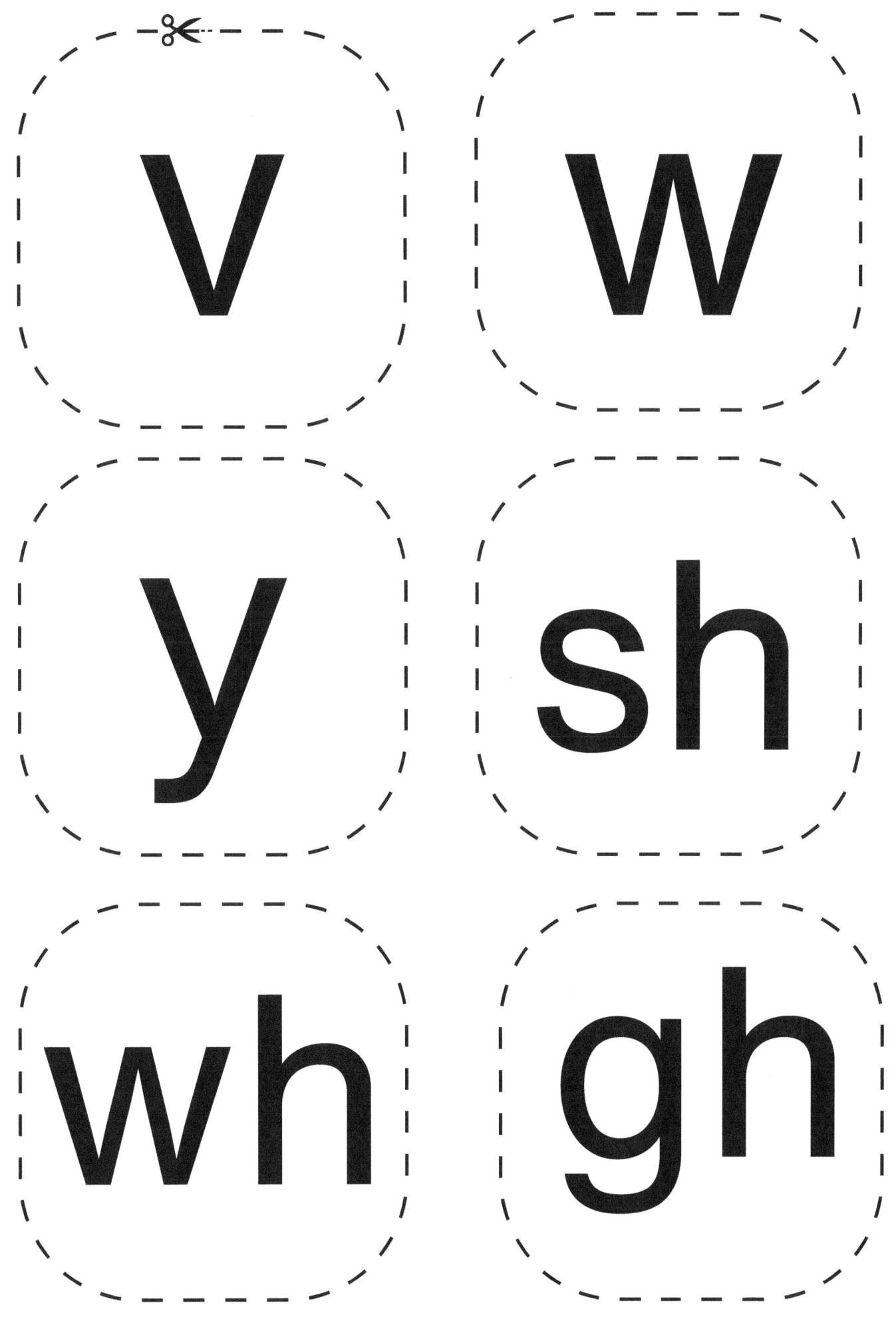

ph

ch

bl

pl

fl

gl

gr

pr

tr

sm

sw

fr

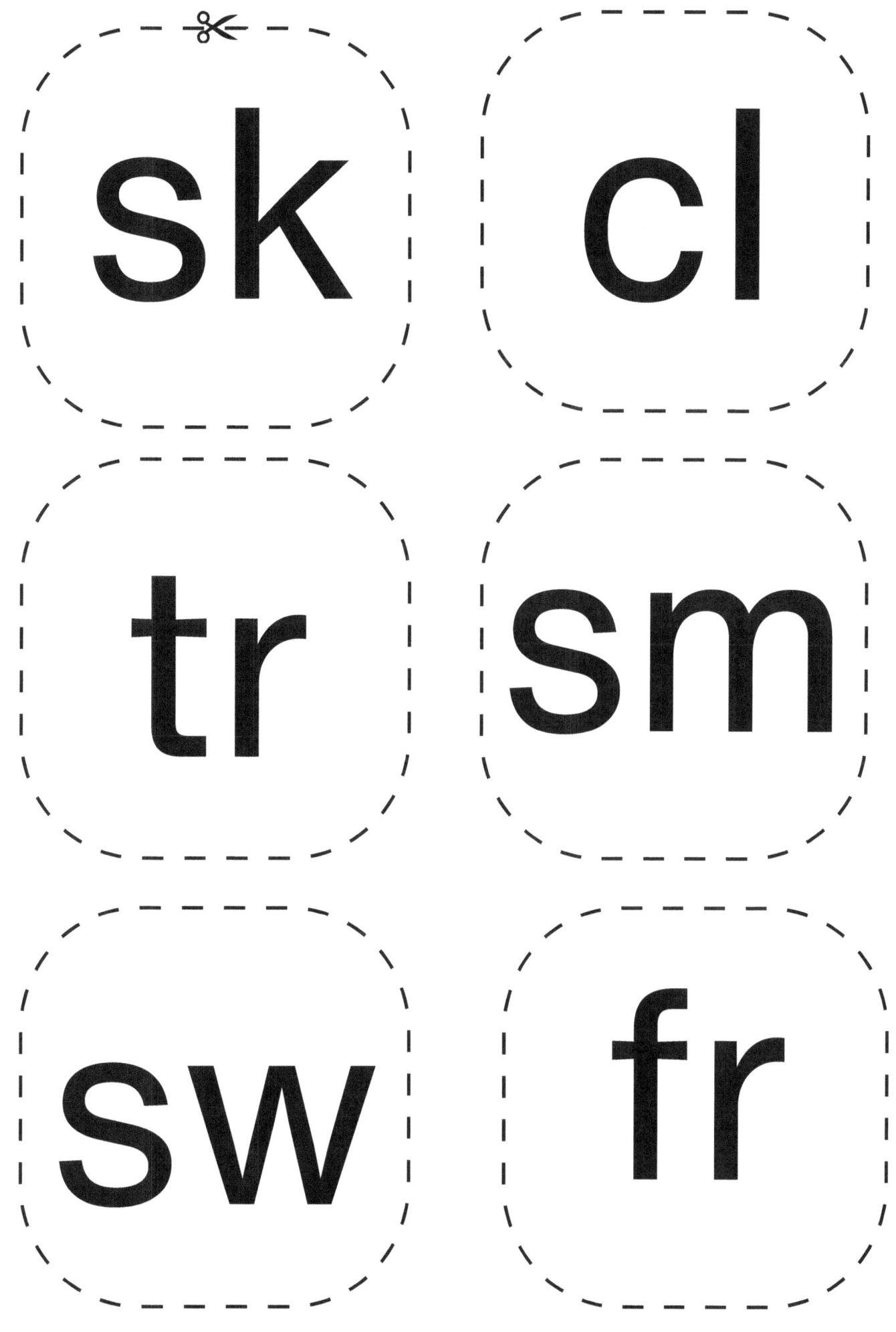

WORD BUILDING ACTIVITY WITH WORD FAMILIES/RIMES

Cut out the word family/rime cards and use them in combination with the onset cards to create as many words as possible. You can form both real and nonsense words. Start with the word family/rime cards featuring short vowel sounds. Once you're familiar with long vowel sounds, you can then use rimes with long vowels, such as 'ai,' 'ay,' 'ure,' and others.

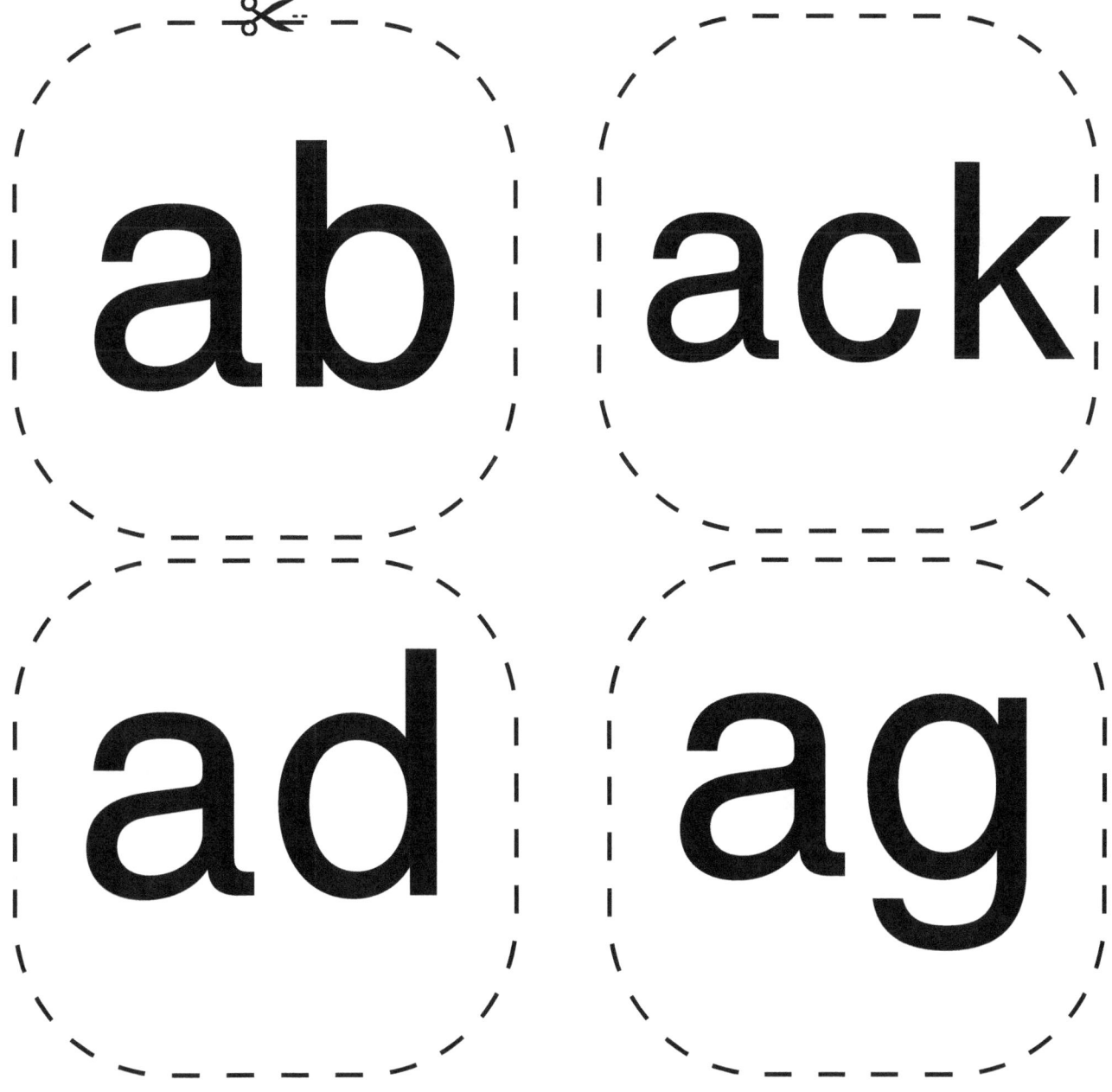

all am

an ap

ar at

aw

ay

ail

ame

ash

ed

eg

eck

ell

em

en

ep

ese

et

est

eve

ey

ib

id

ide

ick

ill

im

in

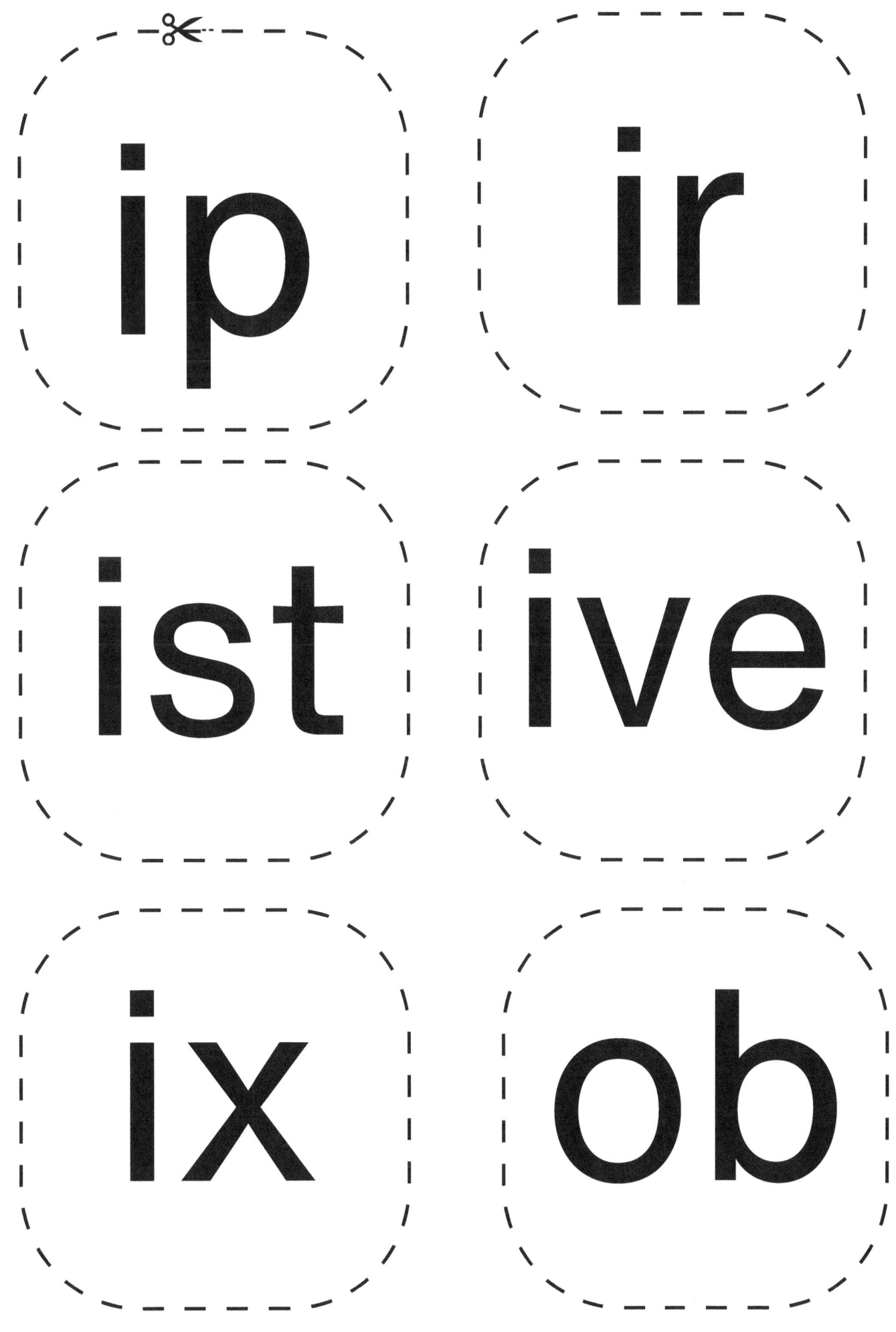

od

ough

og

oke

old

om

one

op

orn

ost

ot

ow

ox

ope

ub

uck

ull

um

un

ust

ut

uge

ure

ean

www.ingramcontent.com/pod-product-compliance
Lightning Source LLC
Chambersburg PA
CBHW080126150626
46550CB00017B/2693